CARRIE'S WAR

Nina Bawden

CARRIE'S WAR

Adapted for the stage
by Emma Reeves

OBERON BOOKS
LONDON

This adaptation of *Carrie's War* was first performed at the Lilian Baylis Theatre, Sadler's Wells on 23 November 2006, in a production by Novel Theatre, with the following company:

CARRIE Sarah Edwardson
CARRIE'S SON / NICK Mark Field
MRS FAZACKERLY Laura Stevely
ALBERT SANDWICH Sam Crane
BILLETING OFFICER / FREDERICK / MR RHYS / MAJOR CASS HARPER Hywel Morgan
HEPZIBAH GREEN Amanda Symonds
AUNTIE LOU / MRS GOTOBED Rachel Isaac
MR EVANS Siôn Tudor Owen
MR JOHNNY James Beddard
MOURNER / ENSEMBLE James Rhodes

Director Andrew Loudon
Designer Edward Lipscomb
Lighting Designer Matthew England
Sound Designer John Leonard
Singing Supervisor Sue Appleby
Fight Director Philip D'Orleans
Casting Director Lucy Jenkins
Company and Stage Manager Lindah Balfour
Deputy Stage Manager Laura Amy Watson
Costume Supervisor Natasha Ward
Producer Mark Bentley

In the West End the show was first produced by Novel Theatre Company at The Apollo Theatre, Shaftesbury Avenue on 18 June 2009 with the following cast:

CARRIE Sarah Edwardson

CARRIE'S SON / NICK James Joyce

MRS FAZACKERLY Ann Micklethwaite

ALBERT SANDWICH John Hefferman

MR RHYS / FREDERICK /
MAJOR CASS HARPER Daniel Llewelyn-Williams

HEPZIBAH GREEN Amanda Symonds

AUNTIE LOU Kacey Ainsworth

MRS GOTOBED Prunella Scales

MR EVANS Siôn Tudor Owen

MR JOHNNY James Beddard

BILLY James Rhodes

MRS DAVIES Holly Boothby

MR OWEN Peter Whitfield

Director Andrew Loudon

Designer Edward Lipscomb

Lighting Designer Matthew England

Sound Designer John Leonard

Singing Supervisor Sue Appleby

Fight Director Philip D'Orléans

Casting Director Lucy Jenkins

Company and Stage Manager Lindah Balfour

Deputy Stage Manager Jo Keating

Assistant Stage Manager Jo Oliver

Costume Supervisor Fizz Jones

Wardrobe Assistant Natasha Ward

Dresser Philippa Gaisford

Accent & Dialect Coach Dewi Hughes

Hair & Wigs Darren Ware

Skull Effect Nick Einhorn

This adaption was produced on a UK tour commencing on 1 September 2010 with the following cast and crew:

CARRIE Sarah Edwardson
CARRIE'S SON / NICK James Byng
MRS FAZACKERLY Ann Micklethwaite
ALBERT SANDWICH Antony Eden
MR RHYS / FREDERICK /
    MAJOR CASS HARPER Daniel Llewelyn-Williams
HEPZIBAH GREEN Amanda Symonds
AUNTIE LOU Hannah Waterman
MRS GOTOBED Brigit Forsyth
MR EVANS Siôn Tudor Owen
MR JOHNNY James Beddard
BILLY Joshua McCord
MRS DAVIES Sarah Lark
MR OWEN Peter Whitfield

Director Andrew Loudon
Set Design Edward Lipscomb
Costume Design Fizz Jones
Lighting Designer Matthew Eagland
Sound Designer John Leonard
Singing Supervisor Sue Appleby
Fight Director Philip D'Orléans
Casting Director Lucy Jenkins
Company and Stage Manager Andrew Jolly
Deputy Stage Manager Irmi Hager
Wardrobe Assistant Freya Groves
Accent & Dialect Coach Sarah Shepherd
Skull Effect Nick Einhorn

Characters

CARRIE

CARRIE'S SON

NICK

MRS FAZACKERLY

ALBERT SANDWICH

BILLY

MR RHYS

MRS DAVIES

MR OWEN

HEPZIBAH GREEN

AUNTIE LOU

MR EVANS

MR JOHNNY

MRS GOTOBED

MAJOR CASS HARPER

FREDERICK

Setting

A multi-locational, multi-level set including a slope (Druid's Grove) and staircase (in the Evans house). The present-day action takes place in Druid's Grove and outside the house, Druid's Bottom. Everything else happens in Carrie's memory. All songs and radio voice-overs are suggestions, subject to copyright approval.

ACT ONE

DRUID'S GROVE

Darkness. The wind whistles through the trees in the grove. Train sound effects. Smoke, as if from a train. Loud train whistle – an unearthly shriek, 'more like a volcano erupting than a steam engine blowing its top'. Mixed in with the whistling sound is a girl's scream. The sound dies away.

Sounds of a summer's day. Daytime, in a wooded, shady place where the light has had to make its way through layers of foliage. Near the top of the slope, ADULT CARRIE pushes through the trees, and enters with a suitcase. She is breathless, as if she has just run up a hill. She is wearing a long, flowing coat. She pauses on the brink and gazes downwards.

The unearthly whistle, not as loud as before – as if in CARRIE's memory. CARRIE shudders, and sways on the brink of the slope. The sound dies away.

CARRIE'S SON enters through the trees, brushing off bits of leaf and twig. He is wearing jeans, etc – 1970s clothes with a strong contemporary feel.

SON: Mum?

CARRIE turns and looks at him blankly.

Mum! How much further?

CARRIE: No further. That's it.

CARRIE points off into the distance, down the slope. Her son looks.

SON: That old ruin?

CARRIE: I forgot – I've been away a long time.

CARRIE wanders down the slope. Her SON sits down on his mum's suitcase, and munches a chocolate bar.

SON: Looks like no one's been here for hundreds of years.

CARRIE: No. No – it's only – (*With wonder.*) Thirty years…

SON: Exactly.

CARRIE: We used to come here all the time, during the war. Me, and little Nick.

SON: Little Nick? What, fat Uncle Nick?

CARRIE: He wasn't fat then. Actually, he looked a lot like you.

CARRIE'S SON offers his chocolate bar to his mum.

SON: D'you want the rest of this?

CARRIE shakes her head. She walks along the top of the bank.

CARRIE: Nick and I used to walk here from the town, along the side of the railway.

SON: What railway?

CARRIE: There used to be a railway. This is the exact spot where the train whistled when it came round the bend. Right by the slope down to Druid's Bottom.

SON: Druid's Bottom?

CARRIE: (*Laughs.*) That's the name of the house. Druid's Bottom. Because it's at the bottom of Druid's Grove.

SON: What's Druid's Grove?

CARRIE: This is. Thousands of years ago, this place was sacred to the Druids. The Old Religion. There's a spring that's supposed to have healing powers, and a stone circle – the remains of a temple. Well, it might be. Albert thought it went back to the Iron Age.

SON: Who's Albert?

CARRIE: Albert Sandwich. He thought there might have been an Iron Age settlement here. He was interested in that sort of thing.

SON: Dad would have been.

CARRIE: Yes. Dad would have been interested, too. Albert and your dad were quite alike. In some ways.

Pause. The stage darkens as the sun passes behind a cloud. A faint, rumbling noise of ancient breathing.

Listen.

SON: What for?

CARRIE: Sometimes – I used to think – I could hear it breathing.

SON: What?

CARRIE: Something old, and huge – and nameless.

SON: (*Unimpressed.*) You mean like a ghost? A monster?

CARRIE: Nothing so simple. Albert said the druids used to make human sacrifices…

SON: You're being weird, you do know that, don't you?

CARRIE: I'm sorry. It's this place…

SON: OK – well, let's go down to the house –

CARRIE: No!

SON: Mum?

CARRIE: Sorry – sorry! I can't. I just can't.

SON: It's all right.

CARRIE: No, it's not all right! I dragged you all this way. I wanted to show you – We were so happy here – I thought – I hoped that would be all I'd remember.

The sound of breathing grows louder.

SON: Mum? What is it?

CARRIE: The last time I was here, I did a terrible thing. The worst thing I've ever done in my life…

SON: What did you do? (*She looks at him, unable to speak.*) How bad can it be? It's not like you killed anyone, is it? (*Beat.*) Is it? (*Beat.*) Who did you kill? Mum!?

CARRIE: (*Snaps out of it.*) Oh, don't be silly, I didn't kill anyone! (*Beat.*) At least – I don't think so. (*Beat.*) I've never told anyone about this… Not even Nick… Not even your Dad…

SON: Well – maybe you should?

Pause. The grove darkens around CARRIE.

MRS GOTOBED emerges from the trees, followed by HEPZIBAH, JOHNNY, ALBERT, MR EVANS and AUNTIE LOU. CARRIE's SON doesn't see them – but CARRIE does – they're crowding into her memory…

CARRIE: You don't change, you know, growing older. I thought I had – that I'd feel differently now – after all, everything's changed – except me… Places change mor than people, perhaps. People…

CARRIE hesitates. YOUNG CARRIE (Dressed in a distinctive coat and hat with her back to the audience.) stands downstage, facing CARRIE. In one hand, YOUNG CARRIE has a suitcase; in the other, a gasmask. CARRIE stares at her younger self.

When she speaks again, CARRIE's voice has a ghostly echo:

CARRIE: (*V.O. AND LIVE.*) …People don't change at all…

FX: The train whistle / scream. As the it dies away, we hear the sound of a steam train gathering speed.

CARRIE exits. Red, flame–like light.

The other characters all melt away, with the exception of YOUNG CARRIE, who remains onstage.

FX: Air raid sirens.

TRAIN PLATFORM

YOUNG CARRIE stands on the train platform (back to the audience).

Also on the train platform (But not with CARRIE.) ALBERT SANDWICH enters with his label, gas mask and suitcase. He sits on his suitcase, takes out a book and reads. Another EVACUEE (BILLY.) watches him.

CARRIE: (*V.O.*) We came here because of the war. The Government sent the children out of the cities, to escape the bombs. We were told to turn up at school with a packed lunch, a suitcase and a gas mask.

YOUNG CARRIE is joined by MRS FAZACKERLY, who gives her a label.

MRS FAZACKERLY: Caroline Willow...

MRS FACKERLY fills out a label for CARRIE during:

CARRIE: (*V.O.*) We were labelled like parcels – but without a destination. Not even the teachers knew where we were going. We weren't encouraged to ask questions. After all, there was a war on. And we were expected to make the best of things.

MRS FAZACKERLY: (*To CARRIE.*) It'll be such fun! Living in the country! You'll love it, see if you don't!

CARRIE: (*V.O.*) But the truth was, we were being sent away, to live with strangers. And nobody knew if we would ever come back...

MRS FAZACKERLY: (*Handing CARRIE the label.*) Put it round your neck, that's right Carrie... and here's one for your brother – (*Looking around.*) Where is Nick?

CARRIE is about to reply when a scuffle breaks out between BILLY and ALBERT. BILLY has stolen ALBERT's book.

ALBERT: Give – that – back!

BILLY: (*Jeering.*) Come and get it!

MRS FAZACKERLY: Billy! Stop that at once! Billy!

MRS FAZACKERLY retrieves the book and hands it to ALBERT.

Whilst this is going on, YOUNG CARRIE goes off to look for NICK, taking the opportunity to swap places with CARRIE.

MRS FAZACKERLY: (*To BILLY.*) You should be ashamed of yourself! Don't you know there's a war on? (*To ALBERT.*) Come with me.

ALBERT and MRS FAZACKERLY go off. BILLY strolls off in a different direction, almost bumping into NICK, who runs in, wearing 1940s-style school uniform, with suitcase and gas mask.

NICK: Carrie!

NICK runs to CARRIE who turns round – we see that she's the original CARRIE, dressed in school uniform.

CARRIE: There you are! Put this on.

NICK: Carrie, I don't want to go.

CARRIE: Ssh. It'll be all right.

NICK: How do you know? You don't, do you? You're just saying that.

FX: TRAIN WHISTLE.

CARRIE: Hurry up. We'll miss the train.

FX: Sound of a train arriving.

CARRIE and NICK move into the train carriage.

TRAIN CARRIAGE

YOUNG CARRIE and NICK are dressed in 1940s-style school uniform. They are wearing labels, have gas masks in cardboard boxes and are sitting in a carriage with their luggage, waiting for the train to depart.

NICK: I don't want to go I don't want to go I don't want to go.

CARRIE: Oh Nick, don't be a baby.

NICK: (*Whimpers.*) I'm hungry.

CARRIE: Eat your packed lunch.

NICK: I've eaten it.

CARRIE: When?

NICK: When you were saying goodbye to Mum.

CARRIE: Nick!

NICK: I was hungry. (*Beat.*) Can I have some of yours?

CARRIE: No!

NICK curls up and feels sorry for himself. MRS FAZACKERLY enters the train compartment, with ALBERT SANDWICH. ALBERT is suffering from a nasty cough.

FAZACKERLY: Here we are! Plenty of room in here!

ALBERT sits down next to CARRIE, coughing. He opens an educational-looking book, and begins to read.

FAZACKERLY notices the miserable NICK.

Poor lamb! You're going to miss your mummy, aren't you?

NICK nods, pathetically.

CARRIE: He's just making a fuss.

NICK: I'm hungry…

FAZACKERLY: Poor love. (*To CARRIE.*) Is there anything for him to eat?

CARRIE: Well, no – I mean, he –

FAZACKERLY: We did tell all the mothers, be sure to provide a nutritious packed lunch.

CARRIE: Here.

CARRIE gives NICK food from her lunch.

FAZACKERLY: There you are – you tuck into that. You'll feel better soon. I'll just check on the others. (*Consulting a list.*) Two Willows, one Sandwich – good.

NICK: (*Mouth full.*) It's not a sandwich, it's a sausage roll.

FAZACKERLY: (*Tousles NICK's hair.*) Get on with you! Look after him, Carrie.

FAZACKERLY goes.

NICK: It's a sausage roll.

CARRIE: I know!

ALBERT looks up. He speaks with a maturity beyond his years. Even whilst conversing, his eyes tend to flick down to his book. He is troubled by a persistent cough.

ALBERT: She means me. I'm Albert Sandwich. (*Coughs.*)

NICK: Albert Sandwich?

CARRIE: (*Nudging NICK.*) Nice to meet you, um – do your friends call you –

ALBERT: What? Jam? Spam? Fish paste? Peanut Butter?

CARRIE: I didn't –

ALBERT: No. They don't.

CARRIE: I was going to say, do they call you Al? Ally? Bert?

ALBERT: I don't care for my name to be abbreviated.

The train whistle blows. Slamming of doors. The train is ready for departure. CARRIE goes to the window.

CARRIE: Come on Nick, wave to Mother! NICK!

NICK joins CARRIE at the window.

NICK: There's too many people, I can't see her.

CARRIE: There she is, over there. Smile!

CARRIE smiles bravely. NICK forces a pathetic smile. They wave. The train chugs out of the station. CARRIE looks at ALBERT, and makes room at the window for him.

Don't you want to wave to your parents?

ALBERT: No point, really. They're dead.

CARRIE: Oh.

CARRIE gives a final wave from the window and sits back down, next to ALBERT.

I'm Carrie / by the way –

ALBERT: Caroline Willow, yes, I know.

CARRIE: How?

He looks at her. She realises, and fiddles with her label.

Oh, yes… Honestly, I don't see why we have to wear these things. I mean, I'm not luggage! I can remember who I am and where I live.

ALBERT: Not if you were killed. That's why we've got them. So that if the train gets bombed, they can identify your body.

NICK: (*Scared.*) Carrie…

CARRIE: Oh, Nick – we won't get bombed.

NICK: How do you know that?

CARRIE: Because – I – well…

NICK: (*Very plaintive.*) I want some chocolate.

CARRIE: You'll be sick.

NICK: I don't care.

CARRIE: All right then.

CARRIE gives NICK some chocolate.

(*To ALBERT.*) He's just a little boy! You could have tried to be tactful!

ALBERT: I was. Actually, if a bomb hits this carriage, there won't be much of our bodies left to identify.

NICK: I don't feel well…

Lights down.

CHAMBERLAIN: (*Voice off, as if on radio.*) …This morning, the British Ambassador in Berlin handed the German Government a final note, stating that unless we heard from them by eleven o'clock that they were prepared at once to withdraw their troops from Poland, a state of war would exist between us. I have to tell you now that no such undertaking has been received, and that therefore, Britain is at war with Germany…

Lights up, dimly: a few hours later. Train sounds. FAZACKERLY enters.

FAZACKERLY: Wake up! We're nearly there! Get your things together – don't leave anything on the train!

NICK: (*Groans, sick.*)

FAZACKERLY: (*Clucks.*) Oh, dear…come here, love.

NICK goes over to FAZACKERLY, just as we hear the loud train whistle. NICK is sick down FAZACKERLY's skirt.

CARRIE: I knew he'd be sick!

FAZACKERLY: (*Dabbing at her skirt.*) Well you might have warned me! (*To NICK.*) Come with me, I'll try to get you cleaned up – (*To CARRIE, as they go.*) Don't forget to bring his luggage when we stop.

CARRIE picks up NICK's gas mask, coat etc. The train slows down.

ALBERT: I suppose this is what they call our ultimate destination.

ALBERT picks up CARRIE's suitcase. Smiles for the first time.
CARRIE smiles back as they make their way onto Welsh soil.

Song: Cwm Rhondda

CHOIR: Arglwydd, arwain trwy'r anialwch,
    Fi, bererin gwael ei wedd,
    Nad oes ynof nerth na bywyd
    Fel yn gorwedd yn y bedd:
    Hollalluog, Hollalluog
    Ydyw'r Un a'm cwyd i'r lan.
    Ydyw'r Un a'm cwyd i'r lan.

TOWN HALL

MR RHYS is ticking off names on a long list. The feeling of a crowded room – MR RHYS takes in the audience as if they're a crowd of evacuees and hosts. BILLY is sitting on his suitcase, waiting.

ALBERT and CARRIE enter, carrying their suitcases and all NICK'S stuff. It's quite a lot for them to manage.

ALBERT: Not much of a place, is it?

CARRIE: It's bound to be dirty. it's a coal mining town.

ALBERT: I don't care about that... (*Struggling with his cough.*) ...But... it doesn't look big enough to have... a decent... library...

FAZACKERLY bustles over, holding NICK by the hand.

FAZACKERLY: There you are! (*To NICK.*) There she is, didn't I tell you? (*To CARRIE.*) Don't lose him again!

CARRIE: But –

FAZACKERLY bustles off. MR RHYS enters with a surly MRS DAVIES.

MR RHYS: (*To MRS DAVIES.*) Rhaid i bawb aberthu! Ma pawb ohonom ni yn y rhyfel hwn.

MRS DAVIES: (*Grim-faced.*) Dim rhyfel ni, yw hwn!

MR RHYS: Duw, duw! Rhyfel Prydain yw hwn, rhaid i bawb neud eu gorau!

CARRIE approaches MR RHYS.

CARRIE: Excuse me...

MR RHYS: Evacuees? Stand over there with the others.

CARRIE: I'm sorry, I don't –

MR RHYS: Just up from London, is it now?

CARRIE: Yes, what do we – ?

MR RHYS: Stand over there and wait for someone to choose you.

CARRIE: (*To ALBERT.*) What's going on?

ALBERT: A sort of cattle market, it seems. (*He puts his suitcase down, sits on it and gets a book out.*) Or a slave auction.

MR RHYS brings MRS DAVIES over to look at CARRIE.

MR RHYS: Now, Mrs Davies – what do you think of this one?

MRS DAVIES: (*Looks at CARRIE.*) Has she brought her own underwear?

MR RHYS: Mrs Davies –

MRS DAVIES: 'Cos I've heard, some of them, like savages they are –

CARRIE: We've brought everything on the list!

MR RHYS: Will that do, Mrs Davies?

MRS DAVIES: I suppose it'll have to. (*To CARRIE.*) Come on then –

NICK: Carrie!

CARRIE: Wait! I can't – not without my brother.

MRS DAVIES: I'm not having a boy.

MR RHYS: He's only a young one –

MRS DAVIES: I'm not having a boy!

MRS RHYS: All right. We've plenty more girls. (*To CARRIE.*) Just you wait over there now.

MR RHYS and MRS DAVIES go off.

CARRIE makes a seat with the suitcases and coats. NICK sprawls over it.

NICK: (*Pathetic.*) Did she get all the sick off my mouth?

CARRIE: Not quite. Come here. (*Wipes him with a handkerchief.*) And try to cheer up! No-one will want us if you look like that!

MR RHYS comes past them.

MR RHYS: Mrs Jenkins is looking for a happy little boy...

He looks at the miserable NICK, and shakes his head.

BILLY grins hopefully at MR RHYS.

MR RHYS: Come with me, son.

MR RHYS takes BILLY off.

Lights fade down.

FX: A few bars of 1940s music.

Lights up again - some time later.

MR RHYS re-enters with MR OWEN.

MR OWEN: ...I want clean ones, mind. I can't be doing with fleas.

MR RHYS: Of course, of course. (*Looking around.*) Two healthy boys to help on Mr Owen's farm? (*Seeing ALBERT and NICK.*) Here we are. Two good... healthy... boys...?

ALBERT is racked with a coughing fit, and NICK still looks nauseous.

MR RHYS and MR OWEN look at each other – and swiftly move on.

Lights fade down.

Sad 1940s music.

Lights up. The MR RHYS comes in with HEPZIBAH.

CARRIE: (*To NICK.*) There's hardly anyone left! Don't blow it this time!

MR RHYS: One for Druid's Bottom... Druid's Bottom... You can't manage two, can you? Are you sure you can't fit two in Druid's Bottom?

NICK begins to giggle. CARRIE puts her hand over his mouth.

CARRIE: Shut up Nick!

ALBERT has another coughing fit. HEPZIBAH looks at him.

HEPZIBAH: Nasty cough you've got there, love.

ALBERT: (*Coughing.*) How very perspicacious you are.

MR RHYS: Now son, we won't stand for your London lip round here –

ALBERT: I was only saying –

MR RHYS: Let's have a bit of respect now! Bit of gratitude. You come down here, expect decent people to take you in – not as if we get a choice in the matter –

ALBERT: And you think I did? (*Coughs again.*)

HEPZIBAH goes over to ALBERT. Puts her hand on his shoulder. He looks up at her. Stops coughing. HEPZIBAH looks at ALBERT's label.

HEPZIBAH: (*Reading.*) Albert Sandwich. Do you want to stay with me?

MR RHYS: You're serious? You'll take this one? Thank you, Miss Green. Just sign for him here, would you? (*Hands HEPZIBAH a billeting notice. Taps ALBERT on the shoulder.*) Off you go, sonny. Mind you behave now.

HEPZIBAH: Come along, love. We'll see what we can do about that cough…

ALBERT goes off with HEPZIBAH.

CARRIE: (*To NICK.*) Well, thanks to you, we're the last.

NICK: Good. Maybe they'll let us go home.

LOU, a Welsh woman with a very nervous manner, enters.

LOU: Mr Rhys… Mr Rhys?

MR RHYS: Ah, Miss Evans! You're a bit late – only two left, I'm afraid! Now, which one would you like?

LOU: Oh, the girl. The girl, definitely.

NICK: Carrie! Don't leave me.

CARRIE: Ssh! I won't. (*To LOU.*) Can't you take both of us, Miss Evans? Please?

LOU: Not a boy. Two girls, perhaps. No boys. I've only the one room, see…

CARRIE: I can share a room with Nick. We don't mind.

LOU: I don't know…my brother's very particular…

CARRIE: Please? We'll be no trouble. I promise.

Pause.

LOU: Well, maybe I can chance it.

CARRIE: Thank you. Oh, thank you.

MR RHYS: Good – that's settled. (*Crossing off his list.*) And that's the last, God be praised.

LOU: (*Hesitant.*) Don't know what my brother will say, mind. Well, I suppose you'd better come home then.

She leads them off.

CHOIR: Hollalluog, Hollalluog
Ydyw'r Un a'm cwyd i'r lan.
Ydyw'r Un a'm cwyd i'r lan.

THE EVANS HOUSE

Auntie LOU leads CARRIE and NICK in.

LOU: (*Nervous.*) Samuel... Samuel?

NICK: (*Calls, helpful.*) Samuel!

LOU jumps.

CARRIE: Shut up, Nick!

LOU: (*Relaxing.*) It's all right, he's gone out to his Council meeting.

NICK: Who's out? Samuel?

LOU: Mr Evans. Councillor Evans.

CARRIE: Your brother?

LOU: Yes... Oh, you will be good, won't you? You look like good children.

CARRIE: We'll try, Miss Evans.

LOU: (*Smiles.*) Call me Auntie. Auntie Louisa.

NICK: Auntie Lou.

LOU: Yes, if you like – but – you'd best call my brother Mr Evans. He is a Councillor, after all. And he's very strong Chapel. So you'll have to be especially good, Sundays. No games, or books –

CARRIE: No books?

LOU: Except the Bible, of course. Best to get these things straight from the start, isn't it? Now, the bathroom's upstairs to the right – hot and cold running water, and flush toilet.

CARRIE: (*Polite.*) Gosh.

NICK giggles and moves towards the stairs. LOU rushes to block his way.

LOU: Wait – before you go up, if you could just change into your slippers –

CARRIE: I'm afraid we haven't brought any.

LOU: (*Embarrassed.*) Oh, I'm sorry, of course, why should you? Wait there now.

LOU goes off. CARRIE and NICK exchange glances.

CARRIE: (*Calling after her.*) Only because there wasn't room in our cases –

LOU reappears with a long roll of white material. She starts to roll it up the stairs, on her hands and knees. CARRIE and NICK watch her as she rolls the carpet up to the landing.

LOU: It's a new carpet, see. Mr Evans doesn't want it trodden on.

NICK: So how are we supposed to get upstairs? Fly?

LOU: Well – of course, you can go upstairs sometimes. Just not too often. So if you could remember to bring down all the things you'll want for the day, in the morning…

NICK: But the bathroom's upstairs!

LOU: Yes, I know bach. But if you want to – go anywhere, there's the one at the end of the yard.

NICK: Outside!

LOU: (*Apologetic.*) Yes… Mr Evans doesn't use it of course, it wouldn't be dignified, not for a Councillor, but I use it – it's quite clean…

NICK looks horrified. CARRIE nudges him.

CARRIE: It'll be fun. Like on that farm where we stayed last summer.

NICK: Spiders! There was spiders!

LOU: God's creatures, spiders. Just like you and me. (*Gesturing upstairs.*) Dere m'lan –

NICK: Not like me! I don't have hundreds of creepy-crawly legs and I don't eat flies or spin sticky stuff out of my tummy…spiders is disgusting, yucky and disgusting…

A door slams, off. LOU freezes on the landing.

MR EVANS: (*Off.*) Lou! Lou! Ble yn y byd ti wedi mynd nawr?

LOU: I'm just coming, Samuel!

LOU scurries down the stairs and off. CARRIE and NICK pick up their bags and begin to creep up the stairs. They pause, halfway up the landing, and listen, as MR EVANS enters and talks to LOU downstairs.

MR EVANS: What are you doing up there? Messing and humbugging about! Wearing out the carpet –

LOU: I'm sorry, Samuel –

MR EVANS: Soon as my back's turned – up and down, up and down – back and forth, in and out –

LOU: Samuel, it's the evacuees –

MR EVANS: Evacuees! I thought we said one!

On the landing, CARRIE and NICK exchange worried glances.

LOU: It's a brother and sister…

28

MR EVANS: A boy! What did I tell you! Can you do nothing right, woman?

LOU: O, paid a bod yn grac. Dwi wedi blino, Samuel.

MR EVANS: Iesu mawr! Wedesi *un* evacuee, a be sy dani? *Dau* evacuee!

NICK: (*Scared.*) He sounds like Hitler!

CARRIE: That's Welsh, not German.

NICK: (*To CARRIE.*) It's just as bad. I want to go home. I want Mum.

CARRIE: (*Holds NICK.*) You've got me. It'll be all right.

NICK: It's not all right! He's a monster! A real life scary monster!

MR EVANS: Be ti'n meddwl bo ti'n neud fenyw! Bachgen, bachgen! Gofyn i ti neud un peth, *un* peth syml. A beth ti wedi neud? Cawlwch!

Sound of Hitler addressing the Nuremberg rally. CARRIE and NICK cling together, scared. Suddenly, the strange sound stops:

MR EVANS: Well, come down then – let's have a look at you.

NICK: Us! He means us!

CARRIE: Come on. It'll be all right.

CARRIE and NICK creep down the stairs, together, and face MR EVANS and LOU. NICK hides behind CARRIE. CARRIE gathers her courage and holds out her hand.

Good evening, Mr Evans. I'm Carrie Willow, and this is my brother Nick.

MR EVANS: Got a bit of manners, I see. That's something! That's a bit of sugar on the pill. (*Inspects the children.*) You've fallen on your feet in this house, let me tell you. You'll get good food here. So no whining round Louisa for titbits when my back's turned! (*Sharply, to NICK.*) Especially you,

29

boy. I know what boys are. Walking stomachs! (*Indicates LOU.*) I told her, fetch a girl now, there's just the one room.

LOU: Samuel, the boy's only a babby –

MR EVANS: Not too much of a babby, I hope. I won't have wet beds in this house!

NICK: That's a rude thing to mention.

MR EVANS: I don't know what you're used to, but this is a God-fearing house. No shouting, no running – and if I hear any Language, I'll wash your mouth with soap.

NICK: We're not allowed to talk? 'Cos I don't know sign language –

LOU: He means, no bad language. No swearing, see.

NICK: We don't swear. Even Dad doesn't swear. And he's a Captain in the Navy.

Beat.

MR EVANS: Then let's hope he's taught you how to behave. It'll save me the trouble.

MR EVANS exits.

LOU: I know he seems – but his bark's much worse than his bite.

NICK: That's 'cos his false teeth are loose.

CARRIE: Nick –

NICK: They are! They click when he talks!

LOU: I mean, there's no need to be afraid of him, bach.

NICK: I'm not scared of anyone whose teeth might fall out. I don't know why you are.

CARRIE: Nick!

LOU: Oh, I'm not scared. Exactly. But I've always – minded him. He's so much older, see, and – when I was young – younger than you are now – our Dad was killed down the pit – and Mammy died not long after –

NICK goes to LOU and hugs her.

CARRIE: (*Embarrassed.*) Nick, don't.

LOU: (*Reciprocating the hug.*) I don't mind!

NICK looks at CARRIE in triumph.

(*To NICK.*) Well, after that, Mr Evans and his wife looked after me, see. I'm not much older than their own son, Frederick… Fred's in the army now, of course. Anyway. Mrs Evans died, God rest her soul, and then it was just the three of us. Mr Evans said we children should be brought up in the fear of the Lord. If Fred was naughty, he'd give him the strap, but me – he'd – He'd sit me on the mantelpiece. There I'd be for hours, my feet pins and needles, scared to death, looking down at the fire…like the flames of Hell it seemed to me…

NICK: That's horrible!

LOU: Taught me to mind my manners, didn't it! You might say he's been more like a father to me than a brother.

NICK: Our dad never sat anyone on a mantelpiece. Or frightened anyone.

LOU: (*Smiles.*) Well, how about some supper, now then is it? There's eggs, milk and bread – and let's see if I can find a couple of biscuits.

LOU takes NICK's hand and they exit together. CARRIE pauses for a moment to take in her new surroundings, before following them. Lights down. Music.

CARRIE: (*Voiceover, stilted.*) Dear Mother, Thank you for the sweets. And the socks. And the letter. I hope you will have a good Christmas in Glasgow. Driving the ambulance sounds very exciting. We were so pleased to hear that you have seen Dad. Please give him our love next time his ship comes into port. You asked us to tell you more about the people we are staying with, well, we are staying with Mr and Miss Evans. Mr Evans is…a Councillor and runs a shop. He lets me help him in the shop. It is – quite interesting…

THE EVANS HOUSE

CARRIE is writing. NICK wanders in, eating a biscuit.

CARRIE: Where did you get that?

NICK: (*His mouth full.*) The shop.

CARRIE: He'll kill you if he catches you!

NICK: (*Swallows the biscuit.*) Too late now. What are you doing?

CARRIE: What does it look like?

NICK grabs the letter from CARRIE and scans it quickly.

NICK: Aren't you going to put about the spiders in the toilet?

CARRIE: No.

NICK: This is rubbish. Boring.

CARRIE: I just can't think what to say –

NICK: You should put, Mr Evans is a mean old pig, and it's freezing all the time 'cos he won't ever put the gas on. And we never get meat, he keeps all our meat ration for himself and we just get his leftovers even though he gets money from the government and Mum and Dad – he DOES! – You told me. And he goes on and on about God and the Bible but he cheats his customers in the shop and he bullies Auntie Lou all the time and makes her cry. And he's got stupid false teeth that don't even fit. That's what I'm going to put, when I write my letter in school.

CARRIE: All right, you write that. And you send it to Mum. And she'll read it and worry and think about it when she's driving her ambulance, and – Is that what you want? Is it?

NICK: But it's true!

CARRIE: Yes, it is. So maybe she'll come and take us away and Auntie Lou will ask why…and she'll show her the letter, and Auntie Lou will cry, and Mr Evans will shout at her and she'll cry again, and –

NICK puts the letter down.

NICK: I just want to go home for Christmas!

CARRIE: Ssh!

LOU has entered and heard NICK's remark.

LOU: I understand, bach. I try my best, I do.

NICK: Oh, it's not 'cos of you.

CARRIE: He just misses Mum and Dad, that's all.

NICK: That's not all.

CARRIE: Yes it is.

LOU: Well. We'll have to try to make it a nice Christmas here. Mr Evans is going to get you a present, you know.

NICK: As long as it's not a Bible.

CARRIE: Nick! (*Politely, to LOU.*) A Bible would be lovely.

NICK: I'd rather have a knife.

CARRIE: You're lucky to get anything at all! (*To LOU.*) Ignore him.

NICK: (*To LOU.*) A penknife like the ones in the shop. In the card behind the door.

NICK cuddles up to LOU, wheedling. LOU bursts out laughing.

LOU: You are a case, Nick Willow!

NICK: I know. What are we having for Christmas dinner? Turkey?

LOU: Goose.

NICK: Goose?

LOU: We always have goose for Christmas dinner. They're fine birds. We get them fresh from my sister's farm.

CARRIE: I didn't know you had a sister.

LOU: We don't see her much. She's not been well...

CARRIE: Where does she live?

LOU: Down at Druid's Bottom.

NICK snorts.

CARRIE: Shut up, Nick.

LOU: Daft old name, isn't it? It just means, the house at the bottom of Druid's Grove.

CARRIE: (*Intrigued.*) Druid's Grove?

The Druid's Grove breathing sound, very faint.

LOU: The deep valley, with the yew trees, by the railway tunnel.

NICK: We picked blackberries there once. It was dark and spooky.

LOU: It's the yew trees make it dark. Funny old place, the Grove. People say it's still full of the old religion – white magic – or the other kind – anyway, it's not a place to go to after dark. Not alone, anyway.

CARRIE: I'd like to go. I wouldn't be afraid.

LOU: You can come with me tomorrow, when I go to fetch the goose. Maybe we'll see Dilys...

CARRIE: Your sister?

LOU: Yes, poor soul, I think of her all the time…

CARRIE: So – why don't you go and see her?

NICK: (*Scoffs, to CARRIE.*) Why do you think?

CARRIE: (*To LOU.*) Mr Evans?

LOU: He won't have it. You see – (*Lowers her voice.*) She married Mr Gotobed, the mine owner's son.

CARRIE: Gotobed. That's a funny name.

MR EVANS enters.

MR EVANS: English! English name, of course. (*To LOU.*) Telling them about Dilys, is it now?

LOU: I was just –

MR EVANS: Have you told them what she did? Dancing on our father's grave!

LOU: Samuel…

MR EVANS: (*To CARRIE and NICK.*) I watched my Dad die. Killed by a rock fall. Need never have happened, if the company had given a stuff about safety. But Mr Gotobed wouldn't spend his precious profits protecting his workers. Always money it was, with that family. Money, money, first and last. Do you know how they made their fortune?

CARRIE and NICK shake their heads.

Slaves, that's how. Sugar and slaves. Human souls meant nothing to them.

LOU: But Samuel…you can't blame Dilys…

MR EVANS: Dilys knew what she was marrying into. Thought she was better than us though she's never lifted a finger in her life. And look where it got her. Her husband died, she's poor and ill – and she'll be alone at the last.

CARRIE: Do you never go to see her?

MR EVANS: Not since she turned her back on her own people.

LOU: I go sometimes – (*MR EVANS looks at her.*) Only to collect the Christmas goose.

MR EVANS: Why don't you send the children this year? Get them to earn their keep for a change.

LOU: They've got to go to school, Samuel.

MR EVANS: They can go after.

NICK: But it'll be dark!

MR EVANS: There's nothing to be afraid of, for those who trust in the Lord.

NICK: But –

MR EVANS: (*Looking at LOU.*) I hope nobody's been putting superstitious ideas in your heads! No wicked pagan nonsense about witchcraft?

LOU looks guilty.

CARRIE: What ideas? Of course we'd love to go. We're not scared of the dark. Are we, Nick?

NICK looks doubtful.

Lights down. The Druid's Grove breathing sound, quietly at first then growing gradually louder.

DRUID'S GROVE

MR JOHNNY enters with a lantern. He looks around before disappearing into the trees.

CARRIE and NICK arrive at the top of the slope. They are carrying a large bag for the goose, between them. NICK stops, forcing CARRIE to stop too.

CARRIE: There's the path down. (*NICK hesitates.*) Come on! What is there to be scared of? Just a few old trees!

NICK: I can hear something.

CARRIE: What?

NICK: Something breathing…

CARRIE: It's just the wind in the trees.

NICK: It doesn't sound like wind! (*Scared.*) Maybe it's a Druid…

CARRIE: Oh, Nick! All that druids and ghosts stuff is just Auntie Lou being superstitious! You know what she's like – she's scared of her own shadow!

NICK: I'm going back.

CARRIE: All right, have it your own way.

CARRIE begins to move down the slope. NICK runs and grabs her.

NICK: Carrie! Don't leave me!

CARRIE: I thought it was you leaving me! Come on…

CARRIE takes a couple of paces down. It grows darker. NICK clings to CARRIE and whimpers:

NICK: Don't leave me!

The Druid's Grove breathing sound grows louder.

CARRIE: Nick?

NICK: What?

CARRIE: I think I can hear it…

NICK: Don't! Stop it, Carrie!

CARRIE: (*Scared.*) It sounds like you said… like breathing…

NICK: (*Really panicking.*) Shut up! Shut up! Shut up!

The breathing sound stops.

CARRIE: It's all right, it's gone. I mean – there was nothing there, really…

NICK: Yes there is…over there, in the trees…

A light shines from the trees. And a voice calls out to them – it's MR JOHNNY, but because of his speech impediment, he's incomprehensible. MR JOHNNY's lines should be very unclear to the audience, so they are given in square brackets.

MR JOHNNY: (*Offstage.*) [Hello! Are you lost?]

NICK: What is it?

CARRIE: I don't know. Who are you? Who's there?

MR JOHNNY enters with a blackout-adapted torch or lamp. He shines the torch on his own face, creating a spooky effect as he tries to explain who he is.

MR JOHNNY: [I'm Johnny. Johnny!]

NICK: (*Wails.*) Carrie…

CARRIE: Come on!

CARRIE grabs the trembling NICK and marches him down the path.

MR JOHNNY: [No, not that way!]

MR JOHNNY cuts down the hill to cut CARRIE and NICK off. He blocks their way. Seeing him loom over them, apparently threatening, CARRIE screams loudly in his ear and runs down the slope with NICK. MR JOHNNY holds his ears and rocks to comfort himself. He goes off or hides in the foliage.

DRUID'S BOTTOM – YARD

At the bottom of the slope, HEPZIBAH enters with a lantern. Lights up slightly.

HEPZIBAH: Mr Johnny, is that you?

CARRIE: Help!

NICK: (*Simultaneously.*) Help!

HEPZIBAH: Who's out there?

> *CARRIE and NICK run towards the friendly-sounding adult voice. NICK grabs on to HEPZIBAH.*

NICK: Help!

CARRIE: Help! Help! Please help us.

> *ALBERT SANDWICH joins HEPZIBAH.*

ALBERT: Carrie? Nick?

CARRIE: Albert Sandwich!

HEPZIBAH: (*Calm.*) Ah, you're Lou's evacuees. Come to collect the goose?

CARRIE: Never mind that now! We have to get inside. Something – (*Forcing herself to calm down.*) Something's chasing us. It's still out there, whatever it is.

ALBERT: It?

CARRIE: It – didn't sound human…

ALBERT: Really? (*Calls.*) Mr Johnny! Mr Johnny, are you out there?

HEPZIBAH: Mr Johnny! You come down now!

> *MR JOHNNY emerges and moves down the slope towards them.*

CARRIE: That's it – him!

MR JOHNNY: [She did this.]

> *MR JOHNNY points at CARRIE and screams loudly, impersonating her.*

HEPZIBAH: Yes, yes, I know. It's all right now. Children, this is Mr Johnny Gotobed.

MR JOHNNY: [Hello, hello, how do you do?]

MR JOHNNY holds out his hand to CARRIE. His hand shakes.
She can't bring herself to take it.

NICK: Hello, Mr Johnny. I'm Nick. Nick Willow. And this is
my sister, Carrie.

MR JOHNNY: [Hello Nick Willow and Carrie.]

MR JOHNNY moves towards CARRIE, but CARRIE isn't ready to
shake his hand. HEPZIBAH steps in.

HEPZIBAH: The goose is ready for you. But you'll stop for tea
first, won't you, Carrie?

CARRIE: Oh – yes – Thank you… (*Hesitant.*) Mrs Gotobed?

HEPZIBAH: Bless you, child, I'm not Mrs Gotobed. I'm
Hepzibah Green. I'm the housekeeper here.

CARRIE: Oh. Thank you –

HEPZIBAH: Hepzibah.

CARRIE: Hepzibah.

HEPZIBAH: Albert, take Carrie to fetch the goose while I set
the table. We'll see you in the kitchen.

HEPZIBAH goes off with NICK and MR JOHNNY. CARRIE stays
with ALBERT.

ALBERT: So, you screamed in Mr Johnny's face.

CARRIE: He frightened me.

ALBERT: Not as much as you frightened him.

CARRIE: Who is he, anyway?

ALBERT: Johnny Gotobed.

CARRIE: I thought Mr Gotobed was dead.

ALBERT: Mrs Gotobed's husband is. Mr Johnny's a distant
cousin.

CARRIE: Is he – is he mad?

ALBERT: Mad? Mr Johnny?

CARRIE: Well, is he?

ALBERT: He's saner than most people. Just a bit simpler than some. Innocent, is what Hepzibah says. She's a witch, by the way.

CARRIE: (*Taking a step away.*) There's no such thing –

ALBERT: (*Grabs CARRIE's arm.*) Carrie, look out!

CARRIE: What? What is it?

ALBERT: You almost fell in the horse pond, that's all. It's quite dangerous in the blackout.

CARRIE: Why, how deep is it?

ALBERT: (*Serious.*) Bottomless. That's what Hepzibah told me.

CARRIE: You're just trying to scare me.

ALBERT: Oh, there's really nothing to be afraid of here. Come on, I'll show you the library.

CARRIE: The library?

ALBERT: You'll like it. It's where we keep the Screaming Skull.

ALBERT goes off. Left alone in the looming shadows, CARRIE hesitates and then follows. The Druid's Grove breathing sound.

DRUID'S BOTTOM – LIBRARY

ALBERT shows CARRIE around the library. The screaming skull is on a shelf.

ALBERT: It's a proper library – in a house! Marvellous, isn't it?

CARRIE: Is this the – the Screaming Skull?

ALBERT: What do you think?

CARRIE: It's horrible.

ALBERT: It's only a skull. We've all got one.

CARRIE: Yes, inside our heads! Covered with eyes, and hair, and skin, and –

ALBERT: (*Grins.*) Touch it. Go on.

CARRIE reaches out to the skull, hesitantly.

CARRIE: It feels – warm… (*Remembers and moves her hand away.*) Why do you call it the Screaming Skull?

ALBERT: It's an old story. You'd better ask Hepzibah – she tells it better than I can.

CARRIE: You said she was a witch…

ALBERT: Not what you're thinking. Not black cats and broomsticks. She's more of – a wise woman. You know, I was really ill when I first got here. The doctor thought I was going to die. But Hepzibah whipped up some medicine out of herbs and I got better quite quickly.

CARRIE: So that's where you've been. Ill. In bed.

ALBERT: Why, were you looking for me?

CARRIE: No. (*He looks at her.*) No! And I'm only here because we're supposed to be collecting the goose.

ALBERT: All right. I'll go and get it.

ALBERT puts the skull down, takes the bag from CARRIE's hand.

CARRIE: Albert –

ALBERT: Wait there.

ALBERT goes out. CARRIE waits in the dark library. The breathing sound from Druid's Grove – very faint, this time. CARRIE moves slowly towards the skull. She picks it up. She looks at it, as if imagining the person it used to be. CARRIE becomes aware of another sound.

MRS GOTOBED appears elsewhere in the house. She is wringing her hands. She cries – an even, despairing sob. The sound is quite quiet at first, then grows louder. Still holding the skull, CARRIE moves towards the sound, and jumps slightly as HEPZIBAH enters.

CARRIE: Hepzibah!

HEPZIBAH: I wondered where you'd got to.

CARRIE: I was – I was just – (*Holding out the skull.*) Albert showed me –

HEPZIBAH: The Screaming Skull. Did Albert tell you the story?

CARRIE: No, he – he said you might…

HEPZIBAH: I will – after tea. Come through to the kitchen, now. We've been waiting for you.

HEPZIBAH goes to exit. Holding the skull, CARRIE hesitates, goes to put it back.

CARRIE: I'll just, er –

HEPZIBAH: Oh, bring it with you if you like.

CARRIE: Oh, no. I mean, I –

But HEPZIBAH's gone. Again CARRIE is left alone, holding the skull. She contemplates it for a moment, shivers and goes after HEPZIBAH. Cheerful 1940s music.

DRUID'S BOTTOM – KITCHEN

A warm, safe, lighted place. ALBERT, CARRIE, MR JOHNNY, NICK and HEPZIBAH have finished eating tea. The skull is on the table, near CARRIE. The bag with the goose in it is also in the room. MR JOHNNY talks to NICK with expansive gestures.

MR JOHNNY: [Up in the mountains. They nest in the lake. It looks like a brown island. Then it moves. And you see, it's made of hundreds of baby birds.]

NICK: I'd love to see that. Can we go and look?

MR JOHNNY: [In the spring. I'll show you.]

NICK: I can't wait!

MR JOHNNY: [Would you like to see my cow? I've got a cow.]

HEPZIBAH: Later, I think, Mr Johnny. (*To CARRIE and NICK.*) Have another mince pie now – I'm sure you can manage a bit more!

CARRIE: Oh no, we couldn't eat another thing, thank you.

NICK: I could. I'm starving.

CARRIE: No you're not.

NICK: I am! (*Taking a mince pie.*) This is the best tea ever. We never get anything like this from mean old Evans.

CARRIE: Nick, don't be ungrateful!

MR JOHNNY: (*Imitating CARRIE.*) [Nick, don't be ungrateful.]

NICK and MR JOHNNY laugh together. CARRIE fingers the skull.

HEPZIBAH: Now, Mr Johnny.

MR JOHNNY: (*Indicating CARRIE.*) [She's cross.]

HEPZIBAH: If she is, I'm sure she's got her reasons.

ALBERT: Hepzibah. You were going to tell Carrie that old tale about the skull, weren't you?

MR JOHNNY: (*To HEPZIBAH.*) [Tell a story! Tell a story!]

HEPZIBAH: Are you sure you want to hear it?

CARRIE: Yes… I'd love to. Really.

HEPZIBAH picks up the skull, thoughtfully.

HEPZIBAH: It's an old, old story. I heard it long before I came here, when I used to work for Mr Johnny's parents in Norfolk. They used to tell me about their rich cousins in Wales, and the screaming skull, and the curse on the house. As the story goes, the skull belonged to a little African boy. He was stolen from his home and brought here when he was only ten.

NICK: Why?

HEPZIBAH: It was the fashion at that time, for rich people to have a little black page, dressed in silk and satin, riding on the top of their carriage. So they took this poor innocent, and brought him across the sea, to a strange land. And he cried, as any child would do, taken from his mother. He cried, and cried. The young ladies gave him sweets and toys and made a pet of him, but he just kept on crying. So in the end, they promised him that one day, they would take him home.

CARRIE: They lied to him!

HEPZIBAH: Who knows? Maybe they meant it. But when winter came, the little lad took ill of a fever. He knew he was dying, and it seemed to him that the promise was broken. And he cursed the family. He said, a house built on the bodies of slaves must be forever haunted. You wouldn't let me leave, he said, and now I will stay here forever. According to his curse, if his skull ever leaves this house, the walls will crumble and fall.

CARRIE: Did anyone ever take the skull out?

HEPZIBAH: Oh, yes. Old Mr Gotobed's grandmother once hid the skull in the stable – just to see what would happen…

NICK: What did happen?

HEPZIBAH: Nothing happened all day. But in the middle of the night…

45

NICK: What?

HEPZIBAH: There came a great scream and a crash. All the mirrors, glass and crockery in the house were smashed to pieces. Of course, she took the skull back in at once, and it's been in the library from that day to this. And so, the Gotobed family can never forget that their fortune was made from slavery and death. That was the curse of the African boy. The curse of memory.

Pause as HEPZIBAH's grim story sinks in.

ALBERT: I told you she'd tell it better than me.

CARRIE: It's – a fascinating story…

ALBERT: Yes. It's a lot of old nonsense, of course.

HEPZIBAH: (*Aims a fake blow at ALBERT's ear.*) I'll give you nonsense, my lad!

MR JOHNNY: [It's not clever to make fun.]

HEPZIBAH: That's right, Mr Johnny. Wise people don't mock what they don't understand.

ALBERT takes the skull and shows it to CARRIE.

ALBERT: But I do understand – look, it's got wisdom teeth – you don't get those till you're eighteen at least. But it's too small for an adult male so it must be a woman. I think it came from an iron age settlement at the top of the Grove. I'd like to take it to the British Museum one day and get them to test its age. What do you think?

CARRIE: I think…that would spoil the story.

MR JOHNNY: [Tell a story. Tell a story.]

HEPZIBAH: (*Teasing.*) Mr Johnny, you've got more sense in your little finger than he's got in his clever young head.

ALBERT: (*Smiles.*) I'm sorry, Hepzibah. You do tell a wonderful story.

MR JOHNNY: [Tell a story.]

NICK: Tell us another one.

CARRIE: We can't – I mean, we ought to go, really. It's getting late and Auntie Lou will be worried.

NICK: I don't want to go! I want to stay here, with you.

HEPZIBAH: You can come back, love. Both of you, whenever you like.

CARRIE: (*To NICK.*) There we are. That's something to look forward to, isn't it?

NICK: I don't want to look forward. I don't want to go back to old Evans.

CARRIE: Well, we have to.

ALBERT: I'll come with you if you like. As far as the railway.

HEPZIBAH: Not with your chest, you won't.

ALBERT: I can't exactly leave it behind.

HEPZIBAH: I mean, you shouldn't go out in the night air, Mr Clever Clogs.

MR JOHNNY: [I'll come with you. I'll show you.]

HEPZIBAH: There you are, Mr Johnny will see you safe through the Grove.

CARRIE: Oh… Thank you, Mr Johnny.

CARRIE smiles and holds her hand out to MR JOHNNY. He puts his hands over his face and backs away.

NICK: Don't look straight at him like that! He doesn't like being stared at. Come on, Mr Johnny.

MR JOHNNY goes out with NICK.

CARRIE: (*Awkward.*) Goodbye, Hepzibah. Thank you for a lovely tea.

ALBERT helps CARRIE with the goose in the bag.

ALBERT: I'll just see you to the front door.

HEPZIBAH: No further, mind. (*Smiles at CARRIE.*) You'll be all right with Mr Johnny. No harm ever comes to the innocent.

CARRIE: Mr Evans says, no harm ever comes to those who trust in the Lord.

HEPZIBAH: Maybe that's another way of saying the same thing.

CARRIE and ALBERT go out. 1940s Christmas music on radio.

THE EVANS HOUSE

CARRIE and NICK watch as LOU examines the goose.

LOU: My, it's a fine bird. Hepzibah Green's a rare hand with poultry. (*Seeing MR EVANS enter.*) Look, Samuel –

MR EVANS stamps in.

MR EVANS: Back at last, is it now? (*To CARRIE.*) Well? How's my sister? That woman looking after her, is she?

CARRIE: Good evening, Mr Evans. I'm afraid we didn't see your sister.

MR EVANS: Well, you stayed long enough. (*Looks closely at CARRIE.*) Have a good time, did you?

CARRIE: It was all right, thank you for asking.

NICK: All right? It was smashing. The house was haunted, and we saw the Screaming Skull, and Hepzibah made us the best tea –

MR EVANS: Better than you get here, I suppose?

CARRIE: No –

NICK: (*Simultaneously.*) Yes –

Pause.

LOU: (*Of the goose.*) I'll just pop this in the pantry.

She exits. CARRIE gives NICK a stern look.

NICK: (*To CARRIE.*) What?

MR EVANS: So Hepzibah Green fed you well.

NICK: We had pies, and eggs, and ham. Meat. Loads of meat.

MR EVANS: Easy to be generous, when you don't foot the bill!
Hepzibah Green's onto a good thing. A mistress too ill to
keep her eye on the books! Feathering her own nest, no
doubt. Taking a little here and a little there, whenever she
gets the chance –

NICK: Hepzibah isn't a thief! She's kind, and she never bullies
anyone or goes on about the Bible and you can go upstairs
as much as you like and there are no spiders and –

CARRIE: Nick!

MR EVANS: I suppose you'd rather be living there with her,
would you?

NICK begins to reply, but CARRIE interrupts.

CARRIE: Well, Hepzibah's quite nice. But the house is so old,
and dark, and we were a bit scared of Mr Johnny!

NICK: (*Shocked.*) Carrie!

MR EVANS: So, you saw the idiot, did you?

CARRIE: I – er –

NICK: (*Simultaneously.*) Mr Johnny's not an idiot, he's not!
You're an idiot if you think that –

CARRIE: Nick! (*To MR EVANS.*) He doesn't mean it. He's just
tired after the walk.

NICK: No I'm not!

MR EVANS: Too much rich food, that's what it is. Boys shouldn't have meat, it makes them boisterous.

NICK: You're an idiot, and a mean old beast –

CARRIE: Nick, go to bed now!

NICK: Carrie Willow, you horrible, ugly cow.

NICK runs up the stairs.

CARRIE: *(To MR EVANS.)* I'm sorry. I'll put him to bed.

NICK: I'm not a baby!

MR EVANS: You make sure you do, Carrie. No supper tonight, mind!

MR EVANS goes out. CARRIE follows NICK onto the stairs, where he's fighting back tears.

CARRIE: Come on, Nick. Go up to bed…

NICK: I'm not speaking to you.

CARRIE: What did I do?

NICK: You're worse than him. He hates everyone, but you're nasty about people you like – just to suck up to him. Saying Hepzibah was quite nice!

CARRIE: We hardly know her!

NICK: I do! I love Hepzibah, and you just stood there and let Mr Evans call her a thief…

CARRIE: You know what Mr Evans is like! If he thinks we like Hepzibah, and Mr Johnny, he'll never let us go there again. He hates to see anyone enjoying anything. It – makes him jealous.

NICK: Just like you, then.

CARRIE: That's not fair.

NICK: Like you know about being fair. Traitor.

CARRIE: I think you'd better go to bed.

> *CARRIE tries to put her arm around NICK.*

NICK: Don't touch me. Don't talk to me. Don't even look at me. You filthy traitor.

CARRIE: Oh Nick, don't be silly.

NICK: Listen to yourself! Why don't you just go downstairs and suck up to your best friend Mr Evans?

> *NICK runs up to the bedroom and flings himself down on the bed. CARRIE sits on the stairs and thinks. The stage grows darker. LOU and MR EVANS enter downstairs, talking.*

MR EVANS: All I'm saying is, it might be an idea to get her to go there sometimes, keep her eyes open.

LOU: Samuel, we can't set the child spying –

MR EVANS: Spying! What sort of a word is that? Keep her eyes open, that's all I said! It's Dilys I'm thinking of – Dilys, our own flesh and blood.

LOU: That's the first time I've heard you say it, in many a long year.

> *CARRIE, listening, makes her way down the stairs to the front room.*

MR EVANS: Well. It was one thing, when she had her pride and strength. But that's gone from her now – and it hurts me, to think of her, helpless in that woman's power.

CARRIE: What woman's power?

MR EVANS: What are you doing, girl? I thought you went to bed! Up and down, up and down, tramp, tramp on the carpet!

CARRIE: I walked on the paint!

MR EVANS: All right, all right, girl. Come here girl, sit down. I know you've got your head screwed on. I was saying to Lou, she's a smart girl. Not one to be taken in by lies and soft, smarmy ways.

CARRIE: Are you talking about Hepzibah Green?

MR EVANS: There, I knew you'd see through her!

LOU: Samuel…

MR EVANS: Be quiet, Lou, I'm only asking the girl! When you were up at my sister's house today, did you see or hear – anything suspicious? Or unusual?

CARRIE hesitates. In Druid's Grove, we see MRS GOTOBED and HEAR the sound of her sobbing.

CARRIE: (*Hesitates, then.*) No. Nothing.

MR EVANS looks at CARRIE.

MR EVANS: Very good then. Just you let me know if you do.

CARRIE: Hepzibah said we could go to Druid's Bottom as often as we liked…?

MR EVANS: There you are then. I knew you'd keep your eyes open for me.

CARRIE: Yes.

MR EVANS: You're a good girl. Up you go now. Time for bed.

LOU: Nos da, cariad.

MR EVANS: Nos da.

CARRIE: Nos da.

CARRIE goes upstairs.

THE EVANS HOUSE

Night in the Evans house. Darkness.

Song: Ar Hyd Y Nos

During the song, NICK *appears at the top of the stairs.*

CHOIR: Holl amrantau'r sêr ddywedant
Ar hyd y nos.
Dyma'r ffordd i fro gogoniant
Ar hyd y nos.

NICK creeps down the stairs.

Golau arall yw tywyllwch,
I arddangos gwir brydferthwch,
Teulu'r nefoedd mewn tawelwch
Ar hyd y nos.

NICK reaches the bottom of the stairs and exits. CARRIE *enters, wearing a dressing gown.*

CARRIE: (*Whispers.*) Nick? Nick?

NICK re-enters, holding a tin behind his back.

NICK: (*Whispers.*) Carrie?

CARRIE: (*Whispers.*) What are you doing? You're not running away are you?

NICK: (*Whispers.*) No.

CARRIE: (*Whispers.*) I'm sorry I upset you. I didn't mean to.

NICK: (*Whispers.*) It doesn't matter. Go back to bed.

CARRIE: What are you doing?

NICK moves towards CARRIE. Suddenly a light goes on, revealing MR EVANS at the top of the stairs. NICK drops the tin. MR EVANS bounds down the stairs, picks it up and yells in triumph.

MR EVANS: Thief! Thief! Caught red-handed now, aren't you? How long has this been going on?

NICK ducks behind CARRIE.

NICK: Carrie…

A tired LOU appears at the top of the stairs.

LOU: Samuel? Carrie? What's happening?

MR EVANS: What? I caught this boy stealing! That's what!

CARRIE: Stealing?

MR EVANS: My best ginger biscuits! Oh, you'll be sorry, my lad. You'll pay. Asking for the strap, aren't you? Ten of the best on your bare bottom!

NICK: (*Hiding behind CARRIE.*) Carrie!

CARRIE: Please, Mr Evans! I'm sure he didn't think it was stealing.

MR EVANS: Then he'll have to learn to think!

MR EVANS advances on NICK.

NICK: If you hit me, I'll tell. I'll tell my teachers, and the minister, and everyone in Chapel –

MR EVANS: What will you tell them? That you stole? Stole from the good people who took you in?

NICK: I'll tell them I was hungry.

Pause. MR EVANS and NICK confront each other. Then:

MR EVANS: (*To NICK.*) Come here.

LOU gasps and CARRIE is on tenterhooks as NICK approaches MR EVANS, who grabs him by the arm and pulls him down so they're both kneeling alongside each other. MR EVANS takes NICK's hands, and puts them into a praying position. Then MR EVANS begins to pray:

MR EVANS: O Lord, look down upon this sinful child in his wickedness and lead him from his evil ways into righteousness. If he is tempted again, remind him of the pains of Thy Hell, the torment and burning, so that he may quiver in his wretched flesh and repent in his immortal soul...

During MR EVANS' prayer, CARRIE and LOU look on anxiously. NICK, at first, keeps his eyes closed – then peeps as MR EVANS continues to pray with his eyes shut. NICK turns around to LOU and CARRIE and winks / gives them a thumbs up.

Lights fade down.

CHOIR: Golau arall yw tywyllwch,
    I arddangos gwir brydferthwch,
    Teulu'r nefoedd mewn tawelwch
    Ar hyd y nos.

THE EVANS HOUSE – CARRIE AND NICK'S ROOM

CARRIE: I know you weren't hungry. You were just greedy for biscuits.

NICK: Got away with it, didn't I?

CARRIE: He must have prayed for half an hour. I think I'd rather have had the strap.

NICK: I hate him, Carrie. I've never hated anyone so much in my life.

CARRIE: If you really hate it here, we should tell someone.

NICK: Oh, I don't hate being here. I just hate him, that's all. But I like Auntie Lou, and Hepzibah, and Mr Johnny – if he ever lets us see them again –

CARRIE: I spoke to him. We can go to Druid's Bottom as often as we like.

NICK: What did you have to do to make him say that?

CARRIE: Nothing. Go to sleep.

NICK: Carrie?

CARRIE: What?

NICK: Sorry about before.

CARRIE: I'm sorry, too. 'Night.

NICK: Carrie?

CARRIE: What now?

NICK: Thanks for trying to stop him.

CARRIE: That's all right. Just don't do it again.

NICK: Carrie?

CARRIE: What?

NICK: (*Reaches into his pocket.*) Do you want a biscuit?

CARRIE sits up, takes the biscuit and bites into it. NICK grins.

CARRIE: (*Voiceover, narrates.*) Dear Mother, I hope you had a good Christmas. We had a pretty good time in the end. Mr Evans and Auntie Lou were kind enough to give us presents. Nick was given a knife. He was thrilled. I got a Bible, which was very generous of Mr Evans, as I expect when he was young he would have been pleased to get a Bible...

DRUID'S BOTTOM – FARMYARD

CARRIE: (*Voiceover.*) ...You'll be pleased to hear that we're getting lots of fresh country air. We spent most of our Christmas holidays at a local farm, where we've been helping out with the milking and collecting eggs...

During CARRIE's narration, lights gradually up on ALBERT, CARRIE, MR JOHNNY and NICK in the farmyard.

MR JOHNNY indicates to NICK to look under some straw.

MR JOHNNY: [Look under there.]

NICK discovers some eggs with a noise of elation.

CARRIE: (*To NICK.*) What is it?

NICK: Eggs! (*To MR JOHNNY.*) How did you know they'd be there?

MR JOHNNY: [The white hen with the black feathers on her tail. That's her nest.]

NICK: (*Examining the eggs.*) Oh, I see.

ALBERT: (*To CARRIE.*) He knows where all the hens nest, and what time they lay their eggs. Hepzibah says, give him a feather, and he'll tell you what bird it came from.

MR JOHNNY: [The pond's frozen over. I'll show you where you can slide on the ice.]

NICK: Come on!

The gang run off.

CARRIE: (*Voiceover.*) We've made some good friends here, now; Mr Johnny, and Hepzibah, and Albert Sandwich – and of course Mr Evans and Auntie Lou have been very kind. I think we've settled in quite well. In fact, it almost seems as if we've been here for ever…

DRUID'S BOTTOM – KITCHEN

HEPZIBAH is arranging tea-things on a tray. CARRIE and NICK are watching.

HEPZIBAH: How are those chillblains, Nick?

NICK: They're all better now. That ointment you gave me was like magic.

HEPZIBAH: Not magic. Just herbs, and spring water from the Grove.

NICK: (*To CARRIE.*) Auntie Lou says the Grove is magic. Doesn't she?

CARRIE: She doesn't say magic, she says the old religion. It's completely different.

HEPZIBAH: Is it?

MR JOHNNY runs in.

MR JOHNNY: (*To NICK.*) [Johnny's cow's having a baby!]

NICK: Really? Now?

MR JOHNNY: [Yes! Come and see.]

NICK runs out of the kitchen with MR JOHNNY.

CARRIE: (*To HEPZIBAH.*) What's going on?

HEPZIBAH: The cow's calving. I expect Mr Johnny thought Nick would like to watch.

CARRIE: Shouldn't we – don't you need to get a vet or something?

HEPZIBAH laughs heartily.

HEPZIBAH: Leave it to Mr Johnny. He's good with animals.

CARRIE: (*To HEPZIBAH.*) Where's Albert?

HEPZIBAH: Having lessons with the Minister. He'll be finished soon.

CARRIE: Will he?

HEPZIBAH: You can help me if you like.

CARRIE: What are you doing?

HEPZIBAH: Making tea for Mrs Gotobed.

CARRIE: Oh… How is she?

HEPZIBAH: As well as can be expected.

CARRIE: Hepzibah…when I first came here… I heard someone crying. Was it her?

HEPZIBAH: Yes. That would have been her.

CARRIE: Why?

HEPZIBAH: I should think she was unhappy. That's usually why people cry.

CARRIE: Maybe she's lonely. All alone, upstairs…

HEPZIBAH: Maybe… I'll tell you what. I'll put another cup on the tray and you can go and keep her company.

CARRIE: Me?

HEPZIBAH: Why not? You can tell Mr Evans all about it.

Beat.

CARRIE: Let me help you with the tray.

CARRIE takes the tea tray. HEPZIBAH carries a teapot. They go out. Old-fashioned dance music – MRS GOTOBED's favourite dance tune.

DRUID'S BOTTOM – MRS GOTOBED'S SITTING-ROOM

MRS GOTOBED is sitting up, dressed in a ballgown. She has another ballgown on her lap – grey silk with pink feather trim. She holds and strokes it like a pet. She wears a small garnet ring.

CARRIE and HEPZIBAH enter with the tea tray.

HEPZIBAH: Mrs Gotobed, this is Carrie Willow. Carrie, Mrs Gotobed.

CARRIE: Pleased to meet you.

HEPZIBAH sets the tray down. CARRIE hangs back.

MRS GOTOBED: Come over here, pretty child. Let me look at your eyes. Albert says they're like emeralds.

CARRIE: Does he?

HEPZIBAH: Handsome is as handsome does.

HEPZIBAH exits.

MRS GOTOBED: (*To CARRIE.*) Hepzibah thinks looks don't matter but they do, you know. Bring me my jewel box. Table, over there. (*CARRIE does so.*) Open it. Can you find my emerald necklace? I think I'll wear it today. In honour of you, Miss Emerald Eyes.

CARRIE opens the box and hunts through it. There is an envelope in the box, which she takes out and sets aside.

CARRIE: Is this it?

MRS GOTOBED: That's right. Help me put it on. (*CARRIE hesitates.*) Come on! I don't bite, you know!

CARRIE takes the necklace and puts it around MRS GOTOBED's neck.

CARRIE: Are they real emeralds?

MRS GOTOBED: They would have been, once. But they still look the part. That's what's important. Sit down here, child. Do you like my dress?

CARRIE: It's – lovely.

MRS GOTOBED: Yes, it is. My husband gave it to me just after we were married. He loved to buy me clothes. Do you know how many ball gowns I have?

CARRIE: Um –

MRS GOTOBED: Twenty-nine. One for each year of our marriage. There's a green chiffon with pearls around the neck, a red silk, a blue brocade…and I plan to wear every single one, once more, before I die.

CARRIE: Before you die?

MRS GOTOBED: Oh, yes, I'm dying, you see. Pour the tea, child. Did Hepzibah not tell you? (*CARRIE shakes her head.*) Well, I am. Just a little milk for me, and half a slice of bread, folded over.

CARRIE: Would – you like some jam?

MRS GOTOBED: No, child. No jam. (*Sips at her tea.*) So, you're my brother's evacuee. God help you! What do you think of him?

CARRIE: I – like him.

MRS GOTOBED: Then you're the only one that does. Cold, hard, mean man, my brother. (*She nibbles at her bread and butter. Hasn't much appetite. Sets it aside.*) How d'you get on with my baby sister Louisa?

CARRIE: Oh, Auntie Lou's nice.

MRS GOTOBED: Nice, but a fool. Louisa should have got out long ago. But no, she'll lie down and let him walk all over her till the end of her days. Don't you think?

CARRIE: I don't know.

MRS GOTOBED: What about you? Does he walk all over you?

CARRIE: I'm not afraid of him.

MRS GOTOBED: Really? Well, in that case, you can tell him something from me. When I die. (*Looks at CARRIE.*) When I die, tell him that I hadn't forgotten him. That I remember that he's my own flesh and blood, but sometimes you owe more to strangers. Tell him that I've done what I've done because it seemed right – not because I wanted to spite him. Do you understand, child?

CARRIE: I think so.

MRS GOTOBED: Good. Only wait till I'm safely dead first! Or he'll be round here, stamping and yelling, and I haven't the strength for it. Remember – wait till I'm dead.

CARRIE: Yes.

MRS GOTOBED: Now, to important matters. Let me show you my very best dress. (*Holds up the grey silk dress.*) This is silk. Take it, child. Feel it. Stroke it. Real silk – and ostrich feathers. (*CARRIE takes the dress and feels it, obediently. MRS GOTOBED is increasingly sleepy as she continues.*) You know…it

61

was my husband's favourite, you know. He used to say... I looked...like a Queen in it. So I'm saving this one... (*She trails off.*)

CARRIE: Saving it? For what?

MRS GOTOBED: (*Sleepy.*) Saving it till the last...

MRS GOTOBED nods, sleepily. Her eyes close.

CARRIE: Mrs Gotobed?

MRS GOTOBED's head slumps.

Mrs Gotobed?... Mrs Gotobed!

CARRIE runs to the door.

Hepzibah! Hepzibah!

ALBERT enters.

ALBERT: Carrie?

He goes over to MRS GOTOBED.

CARRIE: (*Gestures.*) Mrs Gotobed! She's – she's –

MRS GOTOBED snores.

ALBERT: She's asleep.

CARRIE: I thought...

ALBERT: You thought she was dead?

CARRIE: She told me she was dying.

ALBERT: Oh, she is. Well, we all are, of course, eventually. But she's really dying. She's got a few months to live, at most –

CARRIE: Albert, don't!

ALBERT: Don't what?

CARRIE: Don't talk about it! You're as bad as her. Going on and on about dying –

ALBERT: Maybe she thinks it's important?

MRS GOTOBED: (*Mutters in her sleep.*) Blue brocade tonight I think, with sapphires...

CARRIE: It's horrible. Spooky. Dressing up in all these grand clothes...

ALBERT: That was my idea.

CARRIE: Oh... Why?

ALBERT: It was her life, you see. Parties and ballgowns. When I first came here, she was so miserable. Crying all the time! One evening, she showed me her dresses and cried because she'd never wear them again. I said, why not –

MRS GOTOBED suddenly stirs, and joins the conversation – making CARRIE jump again.

MRS GOTOBED: – And I said, because there's no point. When there's nobody to see.

ALBERT: And I said, there's me. I'd like to see them.

MRS GOTOBED: And so, whenever I fell well enough, I put on one of my gowns, and tell Albert all about the times I wore it before.

ALBERT: It's quite interesing, actually.

CARRIE looks at the odd couple.

CARRIE: You are funny, Albert Sandwich. I mean – not ordinary

ALBERT: I would hate to be ordinary.

MRS GOTOBED: Wouldn't you?

CARRIE: I – don't know...

Lights fade down. CARRIE leaves. MRS GOTOBED and ALBERT stay together, listening to the radio during:

RADIO ANNOUNCER: (*Voiceover.*) From the White House in Washington DC, Ladies and gentlemen, the President of the United States.

ROOSEVELT: (*Voiceover.*) My fellow Americans, it is nearly five months since we were attacked at Pearl Harbor. Since then, we have dispatched strong forces of our army and navy, several hundred thousand of them, to bases and battle-fronts thousands of miles from home...

OUTSIDE MR EVANS' SHOP

A brief burst of American band music, e.g. Bugle Call Rag.

MAJOR CASS HARPER looks around, getting his bearings in the unfamiliar town. He sees NICK go past with his school satchel, and calls him over.

MAJOR HARPER: Hey fella! Can you do me a favour, and tell me –

NICK: (*Interrupts, delighted.*) You're an American soldier, aren't you?

MAJOR HARPER: Now, whatever could have given you that impression?

NICK: Got any sweets?

MAJOR HARPER is puzzled.

You know, 'candy'. Or chocolate, or gum? Come on, you're American, you must have something!

MR EVANS comes out of the shop.

MR EVANS: Nicholas! What on earth do you think you're doing?

NICK: Talking to this American soldier.

MAJOR HARPER: (*Holds out his hand.*) Major Cass Harper. Pleased to meet you.

MR EVANS: Samuel Isaac Evans. Councillor.

Beat.

MAJOR HARPER: OK. You know where I can get a beer, Mr Evans?

MR EVANS: You want me to tell you where you can find a tavern?

MAJOR HARPER: Yeah, is that a problem?

MR EVANS: Let me tell you –

NICK: (*Points.*) The Dog and Duck on the High Street.

MAJOR HARPER: (*Grins at NICK.*) Anywhere I can get a beer that's not warm and flat?

MR EVANS looks at him.

MR EVANS: Try America. Good day. (*To NICK.*) Come along, boy!

MR EVANS goes in. As NICK follows, MAJOR CASS HARPER throws him a bar of chocolate. NICK catches it.

American band music, e.g. Bugle Call Rag, as before.

THE EVANS HOUSE

LOU helps CARRIE try on a dress which is short and somewhat tight.

LOU: I could take down the hem, but still – and it'll need letting out around – around the, the –

CARRIE: Bust.

LOU: Kind of your mother, though. A nice thought. Lovely colour.

CARRIE: Yes.

LOU: Tell you what, bach, if I stitch a bit of cloth into the back, here –

CARRIE: I don't want to put you to any trouble –

LOU: Oh, it's no trouble. You never are, the pair of you. Always down at my sister's place... I hardly see you. Wouldn't know you were meant to be living here, half the time.

CARRIE: Oh, Auntie Lou. It's not because of you.

LOU: I understand, bach. Not much of a home, is it?

CARRIE: Then why do you stay?

LOU: I... Nobody's ever asked me that before. (*Beat.*) I suppose that's the problem, isn't it? Nobody ever asked me. Well, Dilys got the looks in our family –

CARRIE: Oh, no! You're much prettier than her.

LOU: (*Surprised.*) You've seen her, then?

CARRIE: (*Reluctant.*) Once. I saw her once.

LOU: How is she?

CARRIE: She's...got some beautiful dresses...

LOU: They say she's not at all well, poor Dilys.

CARRIE: She's... She told me she was dying.

LOU: I see. Thank you for telling me, cariad. (*Pause.*) Was there any – Did she mention me at all?

CARRIE: She said... Yes. She did.

LOU: What did she say?

CARRIE: She's worried that – She thinks you'll lie down and let him walk all over you till the end of your days. She said you should have got out years ago.

LOU: I see.

MR EVANS enters. They both jump, guilty.

MR EVANS: What's this? Whispering, is it, now? Keeping secrets from me – in my own house?

CARRIE: We're not.

MR EVANS: What's going on, then?

CARRIE: I was just – telling Auntie Lou something Mrs Gotobed said.

MR EVANS: Mrs Gotobed? Dilys? You've seen her, then?

CARRIE: Yes…

MR EVANS: You've seen her and you never told me?

CARRIE: Only once…

MR EVANS: And she gave you a message for Louisa?

CARRIE: Sort of…

MR EVANS: What about me? Her only brother? Was there a message for me?

CARRIE: I – She just… I'm not supposed to –

MR EVANS: Come on, girl! What did she say? What did she say?

LOU: (*Suddenly.*) Samuel, I've had an invitation.

MR EVANS: Invitation? Invitation to what?

LOU: A dance.

MR EVANS: (*Dangerous.*) Dance?

LOU: At the Camp. The American Base, down the valley.

MR EVANS: American soldiers…?

CARRIE: What's wrong with American soldiers?

MR EVANS: You know what they say. Overpaid, overfed, over…here. It's a life of luxury in that camp. Everything laid on for them, handed out on a plate. Food, films, dancing – now women. Our women.

LOU: It's all right, Samuel. It's all done through the Chapel. The Red Cross asked them to find some nice girls –

MR EVANS: Nice girls don't go to dances at American bases!

CARRIE: What's wrong with American bases?

MR EVANS: They're full of American soldiers, that's what!

CARRIE: But isn't it a good thing the Americans are here? To help us fight Hitler?

MR EVANS: You be quiet, and go to your room, girl! I have a few things to say to my sister.

CARRIE hesitates, wanting to be out of it but worried for LOU.

LOU: (*To CARRIE.*) Go on, cariad.

MR EVANS: (*To LOU.*) Sit down. Cau'r drws. Steddu lawr.

CARRIE runs up the stairs. CARRIE and NICK listen as MR EVANS shouts at LOU, downstairs.

THE EVANS HOUSE –
CARRIE AND NICK'S ROOM / DOWNSTAIRS

MR EVANS: Granda nawr!

CARRIE: She must be mad to ask if she can go to a dance. She knows what he's like.

NICK: You are thick. She only did it to stop him bullying you!

CARRIE: Oh, no…

MR EVANS: Dawnsio! Dawnsio!

LOU: Dim ond am un noson, Samuel!

CARRIE: How long will he go on, do you think?

NICK: Just till she cries.

MR EVANS: Byth, byth! Tra bod t'in byw gyda fi!

LOU: (*In tears.*) Pam os rhaid i ti sbwlio popeth?

NICK: There we are. Now he'll make her wash her face, and we'll have tea. Just like usual.

MR EVANS: Cer i olchi dy wyneb.

CARRIE: You've really got used to this, haven't you?

NICK: Getting used to things doesn't make them any better. He's a horrible, disgusting, yucky hog-swine. What was he on at you about? What did he want you to tell him?

CARRIE: I don't know.

NICK: Yes you do. I can tell. So could he.

CARRIE: I…think he wants me to tell him something nasty about Hepzibah.

NICK: Like what?

CARRIE: Like she's cruel to his sister. But that's only part of it… I won't spy for him! I won't! I won't tell him anything!

NICK: Keep your hair on! You don't have to – I mean, he can't make you! Can he?

CARRIE: I don't know. I just don't know.

Music.

End of Act One.

ACT TWO

DANCE HALL

American band music. In Druid's Bottom, ALBERT dances with a frail but happy MRS GOTOBED. Towards the end of the dance, she becomes tired and breathless. ALBERT helps her to sit down and looks after her tenderly. Meanwhile, at the American base, LOU dances with MAJOR CASS HARPER.

THE EVANS HOUSE

A knock at the door.

CARRIE admits MAJOR HARPER. He removes his hat and greets her politely.

MAJOR HARPER: Good evening, ma'am. Is Miss Louisa Evans at home?

CARRIE: Oh – um – I don't – No. Sorry.

MAJOR HARPER: Well… If Miss Louisa isn't home, may I wait for her?

CARRIE: No! Oh, no! You see, she is here, but she's in the shop with Mr Evans. He doesn't like American soldiers –

MAJOR HARPER: I'm a very respectable American soldier.

CARRIE: It doesn't matter. He'd make her cry. He's always making her cry.

MAJOR HARPER: I'm obliged to you for explaining the situation. Perhaps you'd…tell her that Major Cass Harper called. And that I'm real sorry I missed her.

CARRIE: I will.

CARRIE ushers him out. NICK enters.

NICK: Who was that?

CARRIE: An American soldier. Can you believe, he wanted to see Auntie Lou –

NICK: And you sent him away!

CARRIE: Of course! Mr Evans would go mad if he saw him –

NICK: Mr Evans! That's all you think about. What about Auntie Lou?

CARRIE: He'd shout at her and she'd cry. I can't bear it when she cries.

NICK: You can't bear it? So what? Maybe she thinks it'd be worth it.

CARRIE: You're right. Go and get her. Tell her Major Cass Harper's here to see her.

NICK: Where are you going?

CARRIE: I'm going to bring him back.

CARRIE and NICK run off in separate directions.

NICK: (*Calling as he goes.*) Auntie Lou! Auntie Lou!

NICK drags Auntie LOU in. She's carrying a mop and is wearing an old apron.

LOU: What is it, bach? What's all the fuss?

NICK: Your friend's here. Major Cass Harper. He came to see you.

LOU: Oh!

LOU tries to smooth her hair.

NICK: Don't fuss with your hair, it's fine. Just take your apron off, you'll look all right then.

NICK helps LOU to sort herself out as CARRIE runs in.

LOU: Look at me… In my old skirt…

CARRIE: He won't mind that, he's too nice.

LOU: (*Primping.*) Where is he...?

CARRIE: He's in the Dog and Duck, over the road. I told him you'd meet him there.

NICK: (*To CARRIE.*) Nice plan.

LOU: I can't – I can't go into the Dog and Duck. Mr Evans –

CARRIE: Won't know if you don't tell him. Now go!

LOU: I haven't finished mopping the shop floor...

CARRIE: We'll do it.

CARRIE picks up the mop. LOU looks to her, to NICK, to the door, worried.

NICK: Go on! Go!

LOU: I... I... Yes. Thank you.

LOU runs out. CARRIE and NICK look at each other in satisfaction.

CARRIE: Come on, then.

CARRIE takes the mop out. NICK follows. A burst of American band music.

DRUID'S BOTTOM - UPSTAIRS ROOM

ALBERT is sitting with MRS GOTOBED. She seems notably frailer than last time we saw her – no dancing today. They look up as HEPZIBAH shows CARRIE in.

ALBERT: Carrie! We haven't seen you for ages.

MRS GOTOBED: We've missed you, Miss Emerald Eyes.

CARRIE looks at MRS GOTOBED, nervous – taking in her new frailty.

CARRIE: Mr Evans' son has come home on leave...

ALBERT: I see.

CARRIE: I mean – it's been a lot of work. All the extra cleaning, and – cooking –

MRS GOTOBED: (*Imitates MR EVANS.*) "Nothing but the best for Frederick." Don't let my brother work you too hard.

CARRIE: Oh, he's been working too. Tidying the shop – he was poring over the accounts for *hours*. He wants everything to be perfect. So Frederick knows he's got a good business to come back to. After the war.

MRS GOTOBED: And what does Frederick think about it?

CARRIE: I don't think he thinks about it at all.

MRS GOTOBED: Frederick never did. He'll go his own way. Regardless of his father.

CARRIE: That's a shame.

MRS GOTOBED: Is it?

CARRIE: Well – poor Mr. Evans –

ALBERT rolls his eyes.

MRS GOTOBED: A shame for Samuel, maybe. It's all he's ever wanted. (*Imitates MR EVANS.*) You have to leave something behind. To pass down the generations. To your own flesh and blood.

CARRIE realises. Remembers the message.

CARRIE: But – sometimes you owe more to strangers?

MRS GOTOBED: (*Smiles.*) Well remembered.

ALBERT looks at CARRIE, questioning.

CARRIE: Mrs Gotobed gave me a message –

MRS GOTOBED suddenly experiences a spasm of chest pain.

CARRIE: Mrs Gotobed?

MRS GOTOBED can't reply.

CARRIE: Are you – would you like me to fetch Hepzibah?

MRS GOTOBED struggles to breathe. ALBERT supports her head.

ALBERT: (*To CARRIE.*) Yes. Go. Quickly.

CARRIE: Hepzibah!

CARRIE runs off. A pause.

ALBERT takes MRS GOTOBED's hand.

MRS GOTOBED: Albert...

ALBERT: Yes?

MRS GOTOBED: Did I – tell you about – the time I – wore this dress to the Hunt Ball?

ALBERT: Yes.

MRS GOTOBED: (*Satisfied.*) Oh. Good.

HEPZIBAH enters.

HEPZIBAH: Ma'am.

MRS GOTOBED: Hepzibah... Thank you, Albert.

ALBERT: For what?

HEPZIBAH: (*To ALBERT.*) Run along now, child.

ALBERT's surprised, but does what he's told. He leaves – but watches from the shadows.

MRS GOTOBED: Hepzibah... it's time.

HEPZIBAH goes to MRS GOTOBED. She takes the hand of her mistress and old friend, and hugs her with compassion.

Music.

THE EVANS HOUSE

Breakfast. CARRIE, NICK and MR EVANS have finished. LOU hovers nervously, waiting on FREDERICK, who's stuffing his face. He finishes.

FREDERICK: Do us another bacon butty, Lou?

LOU: Another one?

FREDERICK: Come on, Lou! You got bacon in the pantry, I seen it.

LOU: Yes, well, it's got to last us for –

MR EVANS: Give the lad his bacon! We've only got him for a week.

LOU: (*Quietly, as she goes.*) Fortunately.

NICK's amused.

MR EVANS: You coming into the shop today Frederick?

FREDERICK: What you on about Dad? It's Saturday, man.

MR EVANS: Busy day, Saturday.

FREDERICK: I'll come in Monday. Need to get my rest. Supposed to be on leave, aren't I?

MR EVANS: First thing Monday then. You'll see I haven't let things slide. You've got a good sound business here to come back to after the war.

FREDERICK yawns.

Carrie, you'll help out as usual?

CARRIE: Oh – I'm sorry, I can't today.

MR EVANS: Why, where are you going?

CARRIE: Just down to Druid's Bottom. They've cut the hay in the big field, and we promised Mr Johnny we'd help get the harvest in. I'm really sorry – but we did promise…

MR EVANS: Tell you what. Why don't you take Fred here with you?

CARRIE: Um –

FREDERICK: Dad!

MR EVANS: He can make himself useful in the hayfield. Do him good to get off his backside for once!

FREDERICK: I'm all right here.

MR EVANS: I can see that. Sleeping all day, nothing but sleeping and eating. Need to buck up your ideas a bit.

FREDERICK: I'm not going. I'm on leave!

MR EVANS: For your own good, lad. High time you paid your respects to your rich Auntie Dilys. Where there's a will there's a way...

FREDERICK: (*To CARRIE.*) Do you mind if I come with you?

CARRIE: No. Of course we don't mind.

FREDERICK: Tidy.

NICK rolls his eyes. LOU brings in a bacon sandwich. FREDERICK grabs it and stuffs it into his mouth as he goes out. Jolly music, e.g. 'Music While You Work'.

DRUID'S BOTTOM – FIELD

Sounds of a summer's day in the fields. Tired from harvesting, CARRIE and ALBERT enter and flop down. FREDERICK follows with a pitchfork of hay.

FREDERICK: What's the matter with you, Sandwich?

ALBERT: I'm exhausted, that's what. I'm having a rest.

FREDERICK: What are you, nesh?

ALBERT: Quite possibly. I'm certainly not built for physical labour.

76

NICK and MR JOHNNY enter, also tired.

FREDERICK: What about the rest of you? Come on you
'orrible lot, I'm not doing this all myself –

ALBERT: Give it a rest, Freddie. It's nearly dinner time.

FREDERICK: Well, where's the eats?

CARRIE: Auntie Lou made sandwiches.

*CARRIE hands FREDERICK a brown paper package. FREDERICK
puts down the pitchfork and opens the package.*

ALBERT: (*To CARRIE.*) I'm aching all over. (*Referring to
FREDERICK.*) I can't keep up with him. I tell you, Frederick
Evans is not a man, he's a flipping machine.

CARRIE: Not much of a brain, though.

ALBERT grins at CARRIE.

MR JOHNNY: [We should finish today. Your big friend is fast.
Very fast. Very big.]

*FREDERICK is amused by MR JOHNNY's speech. MR JOHNNY
notices.*

FREDERICK: What's he saying?

NICK: Mr Johnny was just saying, thanks for your help.

MR JOHNNY: [Thank you.]

*FREDERICK launches into a cruel and over-the-top imitation of
MR JOHNNY's speech style and mannerisms.*

FREDERICK: [Thank you? That's all right.]

NICK: Don't.

FREDERICK: (*Imitating MR JOHNNY.*) Don't what?

NICK: Don't do that!

MR JOHNNY: [Shut up! Shut up!]

FREDERICK gets up and dances around, imitating MR JOHNNY.

FREDERICK: Don't do what? Don't do this? (*Imitates MR JOHNNY.*) I'm mad Johnny Gotobed, I wear a bow tie in the middle of summer.

FREDERICK reaches out, grabs MR JOHNNY's bow tie, and pulls it.

MR JOHNNY: (*A high, angry cry, somewhere between a scream of rage and a war-cry.*)

As he screams, MR JOHNNY pushes FREDERICK, who falls over. MR JOHNNY picks up the pitchfork. He stands over FREDERICK, threatening. FREDERICK cowers and hides.

ALBERT runs to hold MR JOHNNY back.

FREDERICK: Help! Get him off me! Get him off!

ALBERT: (*Simultaneously.*) No! No, Mr Johnny. (*To NICK.*) Help me hold him!

NICK helps ALBERT. MR JOHNNY responds to NICK.

NICK: It's all right, Mr Johnny. It's all right.

MR JOHNNY: [He made fun of me.]

NICK: I know. I know. But it's all right now. Let's go and find Hepzibah. (*To FREDERICK.*) You're worse than your dad.

NICK and MR JOHNNY leave.

FREDERICK: Did you see that? Did you see what he did to me?

CARRIE: Serves you right.

ALBERT: Carrie –

CARRIE: (*To FREDERICK.*) Serve you right if he'd killed you!

FREDERICK: What did I do? Vicious loony like that. He ought to be locked up.

CARRIE: You ought to be locked up! You dirty bully. You foul, horrible beast.

ALBERT catches hold of CARRIE and steers her away from FREDERICK.

ALBERT: Carrie!

CARRIE: (*To ALBERT.*) What?

FREDERICK looks at ALBERT, and CARRIE, and taps his head meaningfully.

ALBERT: Just ignore him.

CARRIE: I hate him.

ALBERT: I know.

CARRIE: He's wicked. Evil.

ALBERT: No, he's just stupid and ignorant.

CARRIE: I've never seen Mr Johnny so – upset.

ALBERT: Hepzibah says when they lived in Norfolk, he used to get into fights all the time.

CARRIE: Fights? Mr Johnny?

ALBERT: He can't bear to be teased. Really can't stand it. It drives him ma – it sends him into a rage. But he's usually OK now. Druid's Bottom is so out of the way, he doesn't normally meet idiots like (*Indicating FREDERICK.*) him.

CARRIE: Good.

ALBERT: Yes, it is. But…

CARRIE: What?

ALBERT: Well. If they ever have to leave, he might have to be… (*ALBERT trails off.*)

CARRIE: Might have to be…?

ALBERT: (*Low, indicating FREDERICK.*) What he said. Shut up in
– in a madhouse, or something –

CARRIE: Mr Johnny's not mad!

ALBERT: I know. I know! But – you saw what he did just now.

CARRIE: But surely no one would –

*MRS GOTOBED enters, wearing a grey dress trimmed with pink
ostrich feathers. CARRIE grabs at ALBERT's arm.*

Albert!

ALBERT: Ssh!

MRS GOTOBED: Frederick.

FREDERICK: Auntie Dilys?

MRS GOTOBED: Still playing the bully boy, I see.

FREDERICK: It was only a game, Aunty Dilys. A bit of a silly
joke, see.

MRS GOTOBED: You always had a sense of humour, didn't you
Frederick? Didn't get it from your father, did you now?

FREDERICK: Aunty Dilys?

MRS GOTOBED: Are you enjoying your time in the Army?

FREDERICK: Yes, Auntie Dilys.

MRS GOTOBED: And what will you do afterwards? When the
war's over? Will you come back to Samuel's grocery shop?

FREDERICK: It's a narrow place, this valley, Auntie Dilys. Too
narrow for me.

MRS GOTOBED: It'll break your father's heart. I suppose you
know that?

FREDERICK: I want something bigger.

MRS GOTOBED: (*Answering her own question.*) Of course you do.

FREDERICK: Got to get back to the hay, Auntie Dilys. I'll be round on Sunday to say goodbye.

MRS GOTOBED: Goodbye, Frederick.

FREDERICK exits. MRS GOTOBED regards CARRIE.

Now, Miss Emerald Eyes. Do you like my dress?

CARRIE: (*Shaking.*) Y–yes…

MRS GOTOBED: Good. Do you remember the message I gave you?

CARRIE: Yes. Yes, I remember. You hadn't forgotten about your own flesh and blood. But sometimes you owe more to strangers.

MRS GOTOBED takes CARRIE's chin in her hand, examines her.

MRS GOTOBED: (*Kindly.*) Another thing to remember. Things are seldom as bad as you think they're going to be. Not when you come to them. So it's a waste of time, being afraid.

CARRIE: Yes.

MRS GOTOBED exits.

Albert! Did you see her dress?

ALBERT: Yes.

CARRIE: Pale grey silk with pink ostrich feathers…

ALBERT: Yes.

CARRIE: She was keeping that one till last.

ALBERT: I know.

CARRIE: Albert, she's dying!

ALBERT: I know.

CARRIE: I mean, she's going to die soon.

ALBERT: I know.

CARRIE: It's just that... In my whole life... She's the first person I've ever known die.

ALBERT: Well she won't be the last, so you may as well get used to it...

CARRIE: Oh, shut up, Albert Sandwich! Just – shut up!

ALBERT: All right.

ALBERT gets up and leaves, as CARRIE sits down on a bale of hay and weeps. As ALBERT goes, he passes MR JOHNNY.

MR JOHNNY: [She's angry.]

ALBERT: Yes, I know!

ALBERT exits. MR JOHNNY goes over to CARRIE.

MR JOHNNY: (*Makes soothing noises.*)

CARRIE: Mr Johnnny...

MR JOHNNY: (*Soothing.*) Sssh... Sssh...

CARRIE cries. MR JOHNNY hugs and comforts her.

OUTSIDE THE CHAPEL – MRS GOTOBED'S FUNERAL

Song: Calon Lân

HEPZIBAH makes her way slowly through Druid's Grove, singing as she does so:

HEPZIBAH: *Nid wyn gofyn bywyd moethus*
Aur y byd na'i berlau mân
Gofyn rwyf am calon hapus
Calon onest, calon lân.

As HEPZIBAH sings, the rest of the CAST assemble as if at Chapel; MR EVANS, LOU, CARRIE, NICK, ALBERT, MR JOHNNY, MR OWEN, MRS DAVIES and other MOURNERS. HEPZIBAH joins them and they sing the CHORUS together:

THE CHAPEL - MRS GOTOBED'S FUNERAL

CHOIR: *Calon lân yn llawn daioni*
  Tecach yw na'r lili dlos

  CARRIE runs out of the Chapel, crying. ALBERT follows her out.

CHOIR: (*Sotto, during the subsequent dialogue.*)
  Does ond calon lân all ganu
  Canu'r dydd a chanu 'r nos.

ALBERT: Carrie?

CARRIE: I'm all right. I just – had to –

ALBERT: I understand.

  ALBERT sits down next to CARRIE. They listen to the singing for a moment.

CARRIE: It's beautiful. What do you think it means?

CHOIR: *Nid wyn gofyn bywyd moethus*

ALBERT: (*Listens.*) I don't need riches...

CHOIR: *Aur y byd na'i berlau mân*

ALBERT: ...not the things of this world...

CHOIR: *Gofyn rwyf am calon hapus*

ALBERT: I only ask for happiness

CHOIR: *Calon onest, calon lân.*

ALBERT: Of a pure, honest heart...

CHOIR: *Calon lân yn llawn daioni*
  Tecach yw na'r lili dlos
  Does ond calon lân all ganu
  Canu'r dydd a chanu 'r nos.

ALBERT: Only a pure heart can sing – something like that, anyway...

ALBERT looks at CARRIE. Her eyes are far away.

Carrie. It's going to be all right, you know.

CARRIE: How can it be all right? You said that if they had to leave Druid's Bottom, Mr Johnny might have to be –

ALBERT: They won't have to leave.

CARRIE: But Mr Evans will inherit the house, and throw them out –

ALBERT: But he can't. You see, Mrs Gotobed made a will, saying they could both stay on, without paying any rent, as long as they wanted to. So he can't sell the house, or let it, as long as they live. I expect he'll be flaming mad when he finds out. But she felt that Hepzibah deserved it, she'd cared for her so well over the years.

CARRIE: She hadn't forgotten her own flesh and blood. But sometimes you owe more to strangers.

ALBERT: What?

CARRIE: That was what she told me to tell Mr Evans, after she was dead! That she had to do the right thing – to take care of Mr Johnny and Hepzibah. I didn't understand – but now I do. And it's beautiful.

ALBERT: How do you work that out?

CARRIE: Don't you see? She still loved him. Even though they'd quarrelled. That's what the message means.

ALBERT: Does it?

CARRIE: Of course! Because she was thinking about him, even at the end… And she wanted him to know it. To comfort his sad heart.

ALBERT: (*Incredulous.*) To comfort his sad heart?

CARRIE: You wouldn't understand! You haven't got any sisters, or brothers, or – feelings, Albert Sandwich!

The song ends. LOU and MR EVANS enter from the chapel, with NICK in tow.

MR EVANS pauses, as if praying or remembering. Then –

MR EVANS: Well. Thank God that's over.

LOU: It was a lovely service, Samuel.

MR EVANS: Was it?

HEPZIBAH and MR JOHNNY enter.

HEPZIBAH: Mr Evans.

MR EVANS gives HEPZIBAH a frosty nod. MR JOHNNY goes up to MR EVANS.

MR JOHNNY: [Hello, how are you?]

MR EVANS: (*Barks, rudely, to HEPZIBAH.*) What? What's he saying?

HEPZIBAH: Just being polite, Mr Evans. (*To MR JOHNNY.*) Come along. Time to go home.

MR EVANS: Oh, home, is it? And whose home are we talking about?

MR JOHNNY: [Home. Home! Home!]

HEPZIBAH: That's right, Mr Johnny. Let's go now.

HEPZIBAH steers MR JOHNNY off. NICK joins them.

MR EVANS: Who does that woman think she is?

LOU: She was good to Dilys.

MR EVANS: Oh yes, good to Dilys, and we all know why, don't we? Well, I can't stand round here all day, I have a shop to run!

MR EVANS leaves. NICK slips his hand into Auntie LOU's, protectively, and they follow. ALBERT looks at CARRIE.

ALBERT: Ready to comfort his sad heart?

CARRIE: I know how I'd feel if I fell out with Nick, and he died. I'd want to know he was still thinking of me... I expect Mr Evans'll just weep for joy when I tell him.

ALBERT: If you say so.

CARRIE exits, following MR EVANS.

(Calling after her.) But I wouldn't be in too much of a hurry if I were you!

Radio – news of the war. Fades down, continues quietly during the beginning of the next scene.

THE EVANS HOUSE

MR EVANS is listening to the radio and doing the shop accounts. CARRIE enters.

CARRIE: Mr Evans, I've got something to tell you. *(Beat.)* Something important.

MR EVANS turns off the radio.

MR EVANS: Well?

CARRIE: Before Mrs Gotobed died, she gave me a message for you.

MR EVANS: Dilys gave you a message? And you never told me?

CARRIE: No, of course not, she told me to wait till she was dead. Anyway, the message was, she remembered that you were her own flesh and blood.

MR EVANS: I should think so! That it, girl?

CARRIE: No – there was more –

MR EVANS: Well, spit it out then!

CARRIE: I'm trying... She said that sometimes you owe more to strangers –

MR EVANS: Did she now!

CARRIE: – And that she did what she did not to spite you, but because it was the right thing to do.

MR EVANS: Spite me? What did she do to spite me?

CARRIE: I thought you knew…

MR EVANS: Knew what? Come on, girl! What did she do?

CARRIE: Oh, only that she arranged for Mr Johnny and Hepzibah to live at Druid's Bottom for the rest of their lives –

MR EVANS: She – did – what?

CARRIE: But she still left the house to you! It means you can't sell it or let it, but – I'm sure she knew you wouldn't mind. She knew you think things are only worth having if you've earned them yourself. And she thought Hepzibah had earned the right to live in the house, you see…

MR EVANS: Hepzibah. Hepzibah. Hepzibah! (*Towers over CARRIE, threatening.*) So she's got at you too, has she?

CARRIE: I don't understand.

MR EVANS: She's bewitched you with her lying tales and slippery ways. Just like my poor sister. She may think she's done me out of my rights and fixed up a snug home for herself. But I shan't let it lie, she needn't think it. Not if I have to drag her through every court in the land…and believe me, I will!

MR EVANS storms out. A door slams. Pause.

LOU and NICK creep in and see the shell-shocked CARRIE.

NICK: What happened?

CARRIE: Mr Evans…

LOU: What did you say to him, bach?

CARRIE: I – think I've done a terrible thing...

NICK and Auntie LOU look at CARRIE. Lights down.

On the radio, ROBERT DUFF reports on the shelling of an English convoy.

DUFF: (*Voiceover, after an explosion.*) At the moment we can see two bright flashes – three flashes – from the other side of the Channel – and three great puffs of smoke, and now a fourth – at any moment now, shells will be arriving over this side. Four columns of smoke going up on the far side – as the convoy goes past us here – (*Explosion.*) – and there's the – there's the explosion...

DRUID'S BOTTOM – KITCHEN

The Druid's Grove breathing noise continues quietly in the background of the early part of this scene, creating an ominous atmosphere.

HEPZIBAH is decorating an apple pie. ALBERT's reading a book.

CARRIE: (*Calls, off.*) Hepzibah? Mr Johnny?

CARRIE enters.

HEPZIBAH: Come in, love. Nick not with you today?

CARRIE: No, just me. I wanted to know – is everything all right?

HEPZIBAH: (*Busy.*) Of course, why shouldn't it be?

CARRIE: I thought... I wondered if...

Something's not right. CARRIE meets ALBERT's eyes.

ALBERT: We've had a visitor, Carrie.

CARRIE: Mr Evans?

ALBERT: Who do you think?

HEPZIBAH: Only natural that he should want to pay his last respects to his sister.

ALBERT: Respects? Charging into her room and going through all her things? (*To CARRIE.*) That's what he did. Oh, after he told us all to get out in a month's time.

CARRIE: (*To ALBERT.*) But you said he couldn't do that!

ALBERT: Seems I was wrong.

CARRIE: But you told me –

ALBERT: And you told him! Nice work, Carrie! Really – clever.

HEPZIBAH: That's enough! (*Smiles at CARRIE.*) There's no will and that's that. Mr Evans rang the bank and the London solicitors – there's no sign of one anywhere. So, as he's her next of kin – he gets everything.

CARRIE: But she did make a will. She told Albert –

HEPZIBAH: I expect the poor old soul had a kind thought and believed she'd carried it through. She was very sick, you know. So there's no call to blame her.

ALBERT: (*Looking at CARRIE.*) Oh, I don't blame her.

HEPZIBAH: There's no call for blaming anyone. These things happen. (*Picks up the apple pie.*) Now, I'm putting this in the oven. You two make friends by the time it's cooked, or you'll feel the rough edge of my tongue. I'm short on patience today.

HEPZIBAH exits.

CARRIE: Albert, I'm sorry.

ALBERT: Don't apologise to me.

MR JOHNNY enters.

MR JOHNNY: [Hello. Hello, Carrie.]

CARRIE: Hello, Mr Johnny.

MR JOHNNY puts MRS GOTOBED's jewel case on the table.

MR JOHNNY: [Look. Look at this!]

CARRIE: It's her jewel box.

ALBERT: What are you doing with that? You'd better put it away. (*At CARRIE.*) It's Mr Evans' property now.

CARRIE: What does it matter, then? I hope he throws it in the horse pond!

ALBERT: It matters, because your Mr Evans went through the whole house, wrote down everything valuable and told Hepzibah he'd hold her responsible. (*To MR JOHNNY.*) Give it to me, I'll put it back.

ALBERT tries to take the jewel box. MR JOHNNY holds on to it.

MR JOHNNY: [No, no! Listen to me. I've got something to tell you.]

ALBERT: Please, don't be difficult –

CARRIE: He's not! (*To MR JOHNNY.*) You've got something to show us, haven't you?

MR JOHNNY nods eagerly. He puts the jewel box on the table, puckers up his face and sucks his lips.

MR JOHNNY: [That man! Came here!]

ALBERT: I don't understand… Please try harder, Mr Johnny.

CARRIE: It's Mr Evans! His false teeth are loose, and he sucks them, like that!

MR JOHNNY beams at CARRIE. He opens the jewel box, looks around guiltily, pretends to take something from it, puts it in his breast pocket.

MR JOHNNY: [He took it. Took it away.]

ALBERT: Mr Evans was here. And he took something out of the jewel box. Is that it? He stole a necklace? A ring?

MR JOHNNY shakes his head.

MR JOHNNY: [Brown! Brown! Paper! Brown!]

CARRIE: I know what he took! An envelope. There was a brown envelope in here. (*To MR JOHNNY.*) Is that what he took? An envelope?

MR JOHNNY: [Yes! Brown envelope!]

ALBERT: The will! He took her will!

CARRIE: But there wasn't a will…

ALBERT: And that's why everything goes to Mr Evans.

CARRIE: So she made a will, and kept it in her jewel box. Where she thought it would be safe…

ALBERT: If only I'd thought! If only I'd looked, earlier. Before you shot your mouth off and brought that foul man roaring round here.

MR JOHNNY: (*Impersonates MR EVANS.*) [Roaring like this!]

CARRIE: That's not fair!

ALBERT: (*To CARRIE.*) No? I came back early from school today and Hepzibah was crying.

CARRIE: Crying? Hepzibah?

MR JOHNNY: (*Nods and demonstrates.*) [I saw Hepzibah. Crying.]

HEPZIBAH enters.

HEPZIBAH: I was peeling onions, that's all, Mr Johnny.

CARRIE: Hepzibah – do you have to move? (*ALBERT sighs in exasperation.*) I mean, surely Mr Evans can't just –

HEPZIBAH: I'll not stay where I'm not wanted so you needn't think it. (*To CARRIE and ALBERT.*) Now, have you two made up yet?

CARRIE: I don't know.

ALBERT: Maybe.

HEPZIBAH: Well, I don't know which of you is the most stubborn! (*Notices MR JOHNNY playing with the jewel box.*) What are you doing with that, Mr Johnny? Let's put it away, now, shall we?

HEPZIBAH exits with MR JOHNNY, who takes the jewel box.

CARRIE: Surely Hepzibah can get another job?

ALBERT: Yes, but – (*Lowers his voice.*) She's already tried a few places. There was only one farmer who agreed to take in Mr Johnny, and even he wasn't keen. He said he might frighten his wife, or something.

CARRIE: They can't go there, then!

ALBERT: They've got to go somewhere.

CARRIE: (*Thinks.*) If you really think Mr Evans took the will – that's illegal! There must be something we can do.

ALBERT: We'd have to prove she made a will, first.

CARRIE: How do you make a will? Do you just sit down and write one?

ALBERT: No, you need to go to a solicitor.

CARRIE: But Mr Evans called the solicitors.

ALBERT: In London. But what if she went to someone local?

CARRIE: Like who?

ALBERT: Mr Rhys! The Billeting officer. He's a solicitor. Got an office in town –

CARRIE: Well – let's go and ask him, then. Come on! If you really think Mrs Gotobed made a will, let's do something about it.

ALBERT: You're serious, aren't you?

CARRIE is about to answer as HEPZIBAH enters.

HEPZIBAH: My pie's almost done.

CARRIE: It's all right, Hepzibah. We've made it up. (*To ALBERT.*) Haven't we?

ALBERT: Yes.

HEPZIBAH: Glad to hear it.

Lights down.

CHURCHILL: (*Voiceover.*) Hitler knows that he will have to break us in this island or lose the war. If we can stand up to him, all Europe may be freed, and the life of the world may move forward into broad sunlit uplands…

STREET OUTSIDE MR RHYS' OFFICE

CARRIE and ALBERT are waiting. ALBERT looks at his watch.

ALBERT: Five past nine. Maybe he's not coming in this morning – are we going to stand out here all day?

CARRIE: Well, let's go in, and to make an appointment…

ALBERT: Oh yes, that's bound to work. I can just hear them. 'Run away kids, back to your comics. Don't you know there's a war on?'

CARRIE: I thought you wanted to help?

ALBERT: I do – it's just –

MR RHYS walks in, reading a newspaper. He nods at CARRIE and ALBERT and keeps walking.

MR RHYS: Bore da.

CARRIE: Bore da – um, excuse me, er – Sir?

MR RHYS stops, surprised.

MR RHYS: Are you collecting for something? Salvage, is it now? National Savings?

CARRIE: No. We want to speak to you.

MR RHYS: If you're not happy with your billet –

CARRIE: It's not that. We want to know, did you ever work for Mrs Gotobed at Druid's Grove? The lady who died.

MR RHYS: I – advised her on one or two occasions.

CARRIE: What about?

MR RHYS: (*Amused.*) Ah, now, I'm afraid I'm not at liberty to divulge that information.

CARRIE: Please – Did she ever ask you to write a will?

MR RHYS: Now, why on earth would you want to know that?

CARRIE: Because – Albert? (*ALBERT looks away.*) Because he – we think she might have written a will, and then somebody stole it, so – so he could get all her money… (*Trails off.*)

MR RHYS: Duw, duw! I think somebody's been reading too many story books.

CARRIE: It's true! Albert worked it out – didn't you?

ALBERT looks away.

MR RHYS: What you're alleging is a serious crime. Do you understand that?

ALBERT: Of course we do! We're not stupid.

MR RHYS: Well, if you do understand, be careful what you say. There's laws against slander, you know. Did you never hear that careless talk costs lives?

CARRIE: Just tell us if there was a will. Please – we're trying to help some people – it's really important.

MR RHYS: 'Important', is it now? Important? Don't you know there's a war on?

CARRIE: I'm sorry – I explained it all wrong. Albert – you tell him. Please? It makes sense when you say it.

ALBERT: I'm sorry, Carrie. I think we'd better go.

CARRIE: Albert!

MR RHYS: If you really want to help people, why don't you join the Girl Guides?

ALBERT: Carrie! Come on.

ALBERT drags a furious CARRIE off.

The Druid's Grove breathing sound.

DRUID'S GROVE

CARRIE runs through the Grove, followed by ALBERT.

ALBERT: Carrie – wait! Please!

CARRIE flings herself to the ground and sits down. ALBERT joins her.

I know. I know. I'm sorry. Now it's your turn to be angry with me.

CARRIE: Why didn't you fight? I never thought you'd give up so easily.

ALBERT: Do you want the truth?

CARRIE: Yes!

ALBERT: I was scared he'd laugh at me.

CARRIE: That's all?

ALBERT: That's all. I let everyone down because I can't stand to be ridiculed. I'm a rotten coward and I hate myself.

CARRIE: You're not.

ALBERT: Yes, I am.

CARRIE: No, you're not. You're just too clever to rush into things.

ALBERT: Does that make me clever? Or stupid?

CARRIE: It wouldn't have made any difference, anyway. Grown-ups only listen to grown-ups.

The breathing sound, quietly.

ALBERT: Oh, I hate being a kid! You can never make anything happen, or stop anything bad happening. All you can do is stand there and watch and wait to find out what happens. If I was grown up, I could stop this. I could buy Druid's Grove and – we could all live here together.

CARRIE: Me and Nick too?

ALBERT: Of course. That's what I meant.

The sound grows louder.

CARRIE: Did you hear that?

ALBERT: What?

CARRIE: The first time we came here. When we were so scared. It wasn't just Mr Johnny – I thought I heard something else. A sigh. Like someone – something – breathing. Don't laugh!

ALBERT: I'm not. You know there used to be an old temple here?

CARRIE: You said that's where the skull came from.

ALBERT: I was guessing. The temple was just a few stones and some old bones. But they've found similar arrangements all over the world, so they think this religion must have been everywhere once. So many people, believing in something – it must leave an echo, don't you think?

CARRIE: I don't know.

ALBERT: Unless there is something more. Some secret Power, sleeping...

The shrieking whistle as the train goes around the bend. CARRIE and ALBERT jump, and find themselves close together.

CARRIE: (*Laughing but scared.*) It's all right, it's all right, it's just the train. Just the train.

The train noise dies away.

ALBERT: Carrie…

CARRIE turns and sees ALBERT's face close to hers. They kiss.

CARRIE: Thank you.

Pause.

ALBERT: Girls don't say thank you when they get kissed.

CARRIE: How do you know?

Pause.

ALBERT: Carrie…what happens next?

CARRIE: You're just a kid, remember? So you'll just have to wait and find out.

ALBERT: Carrie!

CARRIE gets up. ALBERT grabs her hand, just as NICK runs in, exhausted, having run all the way from the Evans house. He waves a letter at CARRIE.

NICK: Carrie! Carrie!

CARRIE and ALBERT spring apart.

CARRIE: What is it? What's happened?

NICK: (*Tired, panting.*) Letter…from Mum…

CARRIE: Is she all right?

Whilst NICK catches his breath and pants out his story, CARRIE snatches the letter and reads it.

NICK: Yes…better than all right… She's rented a house in the country. She wants us to come and live with her. We're leaving!

CARRIE: (*To ALBERT, flat.*) We're going home.

Lights down.

CHURCHILL: (*Voiceover.*) We shall fight on the beaches, we shall fight on the landing grounds, we shall fight in the fields and in the streets, we shall fight in the hills. We shall never surrender…

THE EVANS HOUSE

MR EVANS finds CARRIE staring into space.

MR EVANS: What's the matter, girl? No call for being homesick now, is there?

CARRIE: I don't know…

MR EVANS: You know, I'm going to miss my assistant. You've been a rare help to me, Carrie. And a better cook than Louisa ever was.

CARRIE: Um – thank you…

MR EVANS: No cause to thank me. (*Beat.*) You may as well have this now. Got a Council Meeting this evening.

MR EVANS reaches into his pocket and gives CARRIE Mrs Gotobed's garnet ring.

CARRIE: It's beautiful. Are you sure…?

MR EVANS: Just a keepsake to remember us by. From your Auntie too, mind. Louisa! Louisa!

LOU enters.

I gave her the ring.

CARRIE: Thank you. It's – very kind of you both.

CARRIE hugs LOU.

LOU: Croeso, cariad.

CARRIE moves towards MR EVANS, to give him a dutiful kiss.
He moves away.

MR EVANS: You be sure to look after it. I'm off to the Council.
Up at six tomorrow for the train, mind!

MR EVANS exits.

CARRIE: Auntie Lou. Thank you so much for – for everything.

LOU: No, thank you. It's been a pleasure, an absolute joy.
(*Hugs CARRIE tightly.*) Oh, there's happy I've been with you
two! There's been life in this house, first time I've known it!

CARRIE: We'll miss you.

LOU: I'll miss you, too.

CARRIE: We'll see you again, one day. We'll come back and
visit –

LOU: Oh, don't bother about that, cariad. No sense looking
back, is there?

CARRIE: I suppose not…

LOU: Put the past behind you. It's the best way. You've got a
whole new life to look forward to. Now, I'm going to cook
you a special last supper – (*Daring.*) Roast beef! Big, thick
slices for all of us. I've kept coupons. (*Sings as she exits.*)
Wish me luck as you wave me goodbye…cheerio, here I
go, on my way…

CARRIE looks after her, nonplussed.

CARRIE: Auntie Lou?

Music: 'Wish Me Luck As You Wave Me Goodbye' by Gracie
Fields.

DRUID'S BOTTOM – KITCHEN

NICK is wolfing down a plate of apple pie. MR JOHNNY is staring at the skull. ALBERT talks to CARRIE:

ALBERT: (*To CARRIE.*) Will you write to me?

CARRIE: Where?

ALBERT: Care of Mr Morgan, the Minister. You write first. Promise?

CARRIE: All right, I promise.

ALBERT: I mean it. You have to write the first letter. And if you don't – I'll know, won't I?

CARRIE: Know what?

ALBERT: I'll just know…

NICK finishes his plate of pie, just as HEPZIBAH enters.

HEPZIBAH: Have you finished that pie?

NICK: (*To HEPZIBAH.*) Can I have one more piece – please? (*She hesitates.*) It's the last time…

HEPZIBAH: I don't want you to be sick on the journey home tomorrow.

NICK: I won't be!

CARRIE: You were when we came here.

NICK: I was not!

CARRIE: Yes you were! And it was all your own fault because you were stinking pig greedy!

NICK: Stinking pig greedy yourself!

MR JOHNNY: [Shush. No fight today. Shush.]

HEPZIBAH: That's right, Mr Johnny. Hush now, the pair of you.

NICK: I'll hush if you'll tell us a story.

HEPZIBAH: Which one? You've heard them all.

NICK: Tell us the one about the African boy.

HEPZIBAH: What made you think of that one?

NICK: Mr Johnny's got the skull.

HEPZIBAH: Mr Johnny!

> *MR JOHNNY looks round, guilty.*

I'll take that, please.

MR JOHNNY: No!

HEPZIBAH: (*Unusually harsh.*) Give it to me now, this minute!

> *MR JOHNNY is upset and holds on to the skull tightly.*

CARRIE: Hepzibah?

HEPZIBAH: I'm sorry. I just don't want Mr Evans to find anything missing. Anything...

CARRIE: I know. Mr Johnny, would you swap with me? I'll swap you the skull for this ring. Look how it shines in the firelight...

> *MR JOHNNY looks, nods approval and takes the ring. He gives CARRIE the skull.*

HEPZIBAH: Carrie – love – where did you get that ring?

CARRIE: Mr Evans gave it to me, why?

HEPZIBAH: No reason. I just wondered, that's all.

ALBERT: May I see it, Mr Johnny?

> *MR JOHNNY gives ALBERT the ring. He shows it to HEPZIBAH.*

It's hers, isn't it?

CARRIE: Whose?

ALBERT: Mrs Gotobed's! The one she wore all the time! Mr Evans stole it.

ALBERT gives CARRIE back her ring.

HEPZIBAH: You can't steal what's your own. It all belongs to him now.

ALBERT: He took it from her jewellery box without asking. (*To CARRIE.*) I wonder what else he took, at the same time?

CARRIE: (*To ALBERT.*) We were right. You were right.

ALBERT: So what?

CARRIE: So what? He stole the Will! This proves it.

ALBERT: Not in a court of law, it won't. Circumstantial evidence. If that.

CARRIE: (*Looking at the ring.*) I never quite believed it until now... He stole the will...! He stole this house!

HEPZIBAH: That's enough talk of stealing, thank you. Do you want the story or not?

CARRIE: Hepzibah –

HEPZIBAH: It's all one to me, but time's getting on and your Auntie will want you back early.

NICK: Oh, she won't mind. Not tonight. Tell us the story!

CARRIE: I'll – just – put the skull back, first... I'll take it to the library...

NICK: Please yourself. Come on, Hepzibah!

As HEPZIBAH begins to tell the story, CARRIE walks out, holding the skull.

HEPZIBAH: He was just ten years old, the African boy, when they stole him from his home, his family, his friends, everything he loved...

Fade lights down.

DRUID'S BOTTOM – YARD

The Druid's Bottom breathing sound, mixed in with various voices over:

HEPZIBAH: (*Voiceover.*) …So on his deathbed, he put a curse on the house. He said, a house built on the bodies of slaves must be forever haunted…

Lights up on CARRIE, alone with the skull, thinking.

MRS GOTOBED: (*Voiceover.*) Tell him that I've done what I've done because it seemed right…

MR EVANS: (*Voiceover.*) She may think she's done me out of my rights and fixed up a snug home for herself… But I shan't let it lie, she needn't think it.

HEPZIBAH: (*Voiceover.*) …it must have seemed to him that the promise was broken…

MRS GOTOBED: (*Voiceover.*) I remember that he's my own flesh and blood, but sometimes you owe more to strangers.

CARRIE stops suddenly by the horse pond, remembering.

ALBERT: (*Voiceover.*) Carrie, look out!

CARRIE: (*Voiceover.*) What? What is it?

ALBERT: (*Voiceover.*) You almost fell in the horse pond, that's all…

CARRIE: (*Voiceover.*) …How deep is it?

ALBERT: (*Voiceover.*) Bottomless….

CARRIE looks towards the horse pond, and draws her arm back as if to hurl in the skull with all her might.

Lights snap out. Sound of a loud splash as the skull sinks into the pond.

THE EVANS HOUSE

CARRIE and NICK enter. There is a note propped up on the table.

CARRIE: Auntie Lou? Auntie Lou, we're back… Where on earth is she?

NICK: (*Grins.*) Who knows? She could be anywhere by now.

CARRIE: What do you mean? Where's she gone?

NICK: Told you, I don't know.

CARRIE: Well, I'd better get Mr Evans' tea on, or he'll be angry.

NICK: Don't bother. He's going to be furious anyway. (*Indicates the letter.*) Soon as he reads this.

CARRIE: What do you mean? Has something happened to Auntie Lou?

NICK: Oh, yes.

CARRIE: Well, what?

NICK: She's run away. With Major Cass Harper. They're getting married tomorrow.

CARRIE: She…? And you knew…? I – I could hit you…

CARRIE chases NICK. He laughs and dodges out of her way. She catches him and lands a pretend blow.

Why? Why didn't you tell me?

NICK: 'Cos you'd have told Mr Evans.

CARRIE: (*Upset.*) Did she think I'd betray her like that?

NICK: She thought you might feel sorry for him.

CARRIE: (*Looks at her ring.*) Well she was wrong. Come on. Let's get out of the way before he comes back. And you can tell me all about it.

CARRIE and NICK go upstairs. The stage darkens. A hint of flickering firelight.

CHOIR: Holl amrantau'r sêr ddywedant
>Ar hyd y nos.
>Dyma'r ffordd i fro gogoniant
>Ar hyd y nos.

>*During the song, MR EVANS enters. He reads the letter. He puts it down. He reads it again. He stares into space / the fire as the stage darkens further.*

>Golau arall yw tywyllwch,
>I arddangos gwir brydferthwch,
>Teulu'r nefoedd mewn tawelwch
>Ar hyd y nos.

THE EVANS HOUSE

Morning. CARRIE goes down the stairs and sees MR EVANS sitting in silence. She watches him for a moment. He doesn't move. CARRIE moves towards him until she is practically standing over him.

CARRIE: Mr Evans?

>*He doesn't respond.*

>Have you been up all night?

MR EVANS: Was just going to wake you. Train goes at seven.

CARRIE: Auntie Lou…

MR EVANS: Gone. Off with her fancy man. Thought you knew.

CARRIE: Are you – angry?

MR EVANS: Ate a lot, didn't she?

CARRIE: Did she?

MR EVANS: Always at it, munch munch, nibble nibble. One less mouth to feed. Fred will feel the benefit, when he comes home to take over the business.

CARRIE: Fred…

MR EVANS: What?

CARRIE: I'm sure you're right.

MR EVANS: One thing riles me, a bit, mind. Why didn't she tell me face to face? Instead of stealing away like a thief in the night –

CARRIE: Maybe she was scared?

MR EVANS: Scared? What's she got to be scared of me for?

CARRIE: (*Genuine.*) I don't know.

MR EVANS: No – she just wanted to make me look small. Like her fine sister, Dilys. Make a right pair, they do, sending messages, leaving notes – look at this, now!

He produces the brown envelope from MRS GOTOBED's jewel box, and opens it to reveal a photograph.

An old photograph! That's all I had from Dilys on her deathbed. No letter, nothing. Just tucked away in her jewel case in an envelope with my name on. This photograph – and that ring you've got.

CARRIE: So that's what was in the envelope in her jewel case? The photograph and the ring?

MR EVANS: Photograph. Ring. That's your lot.

CARRIE: And the envelope had your name on?

MR EVANS: Don't parrot, girl! Yes! (*Shakes his head.*) Thirty years…

CARRIE: Can I see the photograph?

MR EVANS gives it to her.

Is that you and Mrs Gotobed?

MR EVANS: Long time ago now.

CARRIE: She's wearing the ring…this ring.

MR EVANS: I bought it for her with my first wages.

CARRIE: She used to wear it all the time… Until the very end.

MR EVANS: What are you grinning about?

CARRIE: I'm just glad. About the ring and the picture. It means she never stopped thinking about you.

MR EVANS: Seems more like a slap in the face to me. But take it your way if you like. Now get upstairs and wake that idle young brother of yours.

CARRIE: Mr Evans –

MR EVANS: Sharp now, or you'll miss your train.

CARRIE goes upstairs, leaving MR EVANS looking at the photograph.

CHOIR: Nos yw henaint pan ddaw cystudd,
Ond i harddu dyn a'i hwyrddydd
Rhown ein golau gwan i'n gilydd
Ar hyd y nos.

During the song, MR EVANS looks at the photograph for a long time. Then he puts it back in the envelope, puts it in his pocket and walks out. Slowly.

TRAIN CARRIAGE

A guard's whistle. Train sound effects as the steam train chugs through the mountains. Lights fade up on CARRIE and NICK, with their coats and luggage, in the carriage.

NICK: (*Imitating MR EVANS.*) Well. Thank God that's over!

CARRIE: Do you mean that?

NICK: What d'you think? (*Shouts, triumphantly.*) No more Mr Evans! (*Cheers.*) Woo – hoo!

CARRIE: Don't be mean! He was – quite nice, really.

NICK: No, he wasn't!

CARRIE: No, he wasn't. But at least he didn't nick Mrs Gotobed's will.

NICK: What does it matter, now?

CARRIE: I suppose it doesn't. I – just wish I could have told Albert, that's all.

NICK: Albert, Albert. Are you going to write to him?

CARRIE: I don't know. I still can't believe we're going for good.

NICK: We might not. Maybe the train'll get bombed on the way.

CARRIE: It won't. I mean, don't be scared.

NICK: I'm not. I'd like to be bombed, it'd be super-exciting. (*Makes bomb noises.*) Can we have our lunch now?

CARRIE: It's seven in the morning.

NICK: My stomach's flapping.

CARRIE: Just wait till we've gone past Druid's Grove.

NICK: Why? Is Albert going to wave goodbye?

CARRIE: I just want to – say goodbye to the house, that's all.

NICK: Goodbye to the house?

CARRIE: What's wrong with that?

NICK: Nothing. If you're strange. (*Sings, tunelessly.*) Bye bye Druid's Bottom, bye bye Hepzibah and Mr Johnny, bye bye Albert Sandwich, Carrie loves you –

CARRIE: Shut up Nick!

NICK: (*Laughing.*) Carrie loves you –

CARRIE: Shut up! Shut up!

CARRIE puts her hand over NICK's mouth and wrestles him down on to the seat.

NICK: Ow! Get off Carrie you rotten pig –

CARRIE: Serves you right! Serves you –

CARRIE stops still.

NICK: What's the matter? Carrie? What's the matter?

The stage is bathed in a red, fiery glow.

CARRIE stares in horror out of the window. The train whistles with an unearthly shriek.

Simultaneously, CARRIE stands with her face pressed to the window, and screams uncontrollably. NICK is shaken by the sight. Lights down as the train enters the tunnel. During the voiceover, we hear the breathing and heartbeat sound from Druid's Grove, and see MR JOHNNY, struggling as if moving through smoke, calling for Hepzibah and Albert.

CARRIE: (*Voiceover.*) It's on fire, Nick. The house is on fire. Blazing away, flames and smoke – they'll all be dead…

HEPZIBAH: (*Voiceover.*) …if his skull ever leaves this house, the walls will crumble and fall…

LOU: (*Voiceover.*) …Funny old place, the Grove…full of the old religion –

MR EVANS: (*Voiceover.*) …remind him of the pains of Thy Hell, the torment and burning…

CARRIE: (*Voiceover.*) It's burning. They're burning. Hepzibah and Mr Johnny and Albert, and it's all my fault –

LOU: (*Voiceover.*) …white magic – or the other kind…

HEPZIBAH: (*Voiceover.*) …the walls will crumble and fall…

MR EVANS: (*Voiceover.*) …that he may quiver in his wretched flesh and repent in his immortal soul…

CARRIE: (*Voiceover.*) …all my fault…

DRUID'S GROVE

ADULT CARRIE and her SON, as we left them in the first scene.

SON: But it wasn't, was it?

CARRIE: (*Flat.*) See for yourself. It's a ruin. There's nothing left.

SON: I mean, it wasn't your fault. OK, so it burned down. Houses burn down. But not because a girl throws a skull into a horse pond.

CARRIE: I wonder?

SON: Mum!

CARRIE: Sorry. No. Of course. I'm being stupid. Ignore me. (*Smiles brightly.*) All right – shall we head back?

SON: Already?

CARRIE: We should really go and book in –

SON: I think I'll hang out here for a while. If that's OK with you.

Faint breathing sound.

CARRIE: Were you thinking of going down to the house?

SON: (*Shrugs.*) Might check it out – explore a bit – you know…?

CARRIE: I think so. (*Beat.*) Can you find the B and B? We drove past it –

SON: Yeah, it's on, like, the only street in the village?

CARRIE: See you there in an hour.

She ruffles his hair.

SON: Mum.

CARRIE: Be good.

CARRIE smiles and goes. The mysterious breathing sound returns.

SON: Mum?

But she's gone. Slightly freaked out, CARRIE'S SON heads down the slope towards the house.

DRUID'S BOTTOM – YARD

A car drives up, slows and stop. CARRIE'S SON listens. He ducks behind some foliage, and watches as ALBERT arrives and crosses the yard, carrying a suitcase. HEPZIBAH, carrying a basket, comes out to meet ALBERT. They hug.

HEPZIBAH: There you are – oh, it's good to have you back.

ALBERT: (*Hugging her.*) Traffic was a nightmare, as usual. (*Teasing.*) Worth it, though – to see you.

HEPZIBAH: Go on with you, Albert Sandwich.

Surprised, CARRIE'S SON emerges from his hiding place. HEPZIBAH had her back to him, but turns around and speaks as if she's known he was there all along.

Yes, and you can come out now, son. No need to hide from us.

SON: I'm sorry – I thought the house was empty.

ALBERT: So what were you doing here?

SON: I don't know… (*Beat.*) I – I think you knew my mother… In the war.

HEPZIBAH: (*Analyses him.*) Carrie! Carrie's boy! Gracious heavens! Don't you look like –

SON: (*Resigned.*) Uncle Nick, I know.

ALBERT: You're Carrie's son? Carrie Willow?

SON: Yes – I mean, she was, then.

ALBERT: I see…

HEPZIBAH: (*To ALBERT.*) Carrie's boy. Carrie Willow. Well, well…

HEPZIBAH looks at ALBERT – an unspoken question, an expression of regret.

ALBERT: She promised she'd write first. She never did.

SON: But that was because of the fire.

HEPZIBAH: How did she know about that old fire?

SON: She saw it from the train… All these years, she thought you were all dead.

HEPZIBAH: We would have been. Mr Johnny saved us – he woke us all up and got us out. As it turned out, that fire did us a favour. The house was gutted, so we moved into the outbuildings. The lawyers said we could stay on as caretakers.

SON: What about Mr Evans?

HEPZIBAH: He died, poor man. Not long after the fire. His heart, you see. Everything went to Mrs Cass Harper –

SON: Auntie Lou?

HEPZIBAH: That's right, yes, Louisa, and she let us stay on – until Albert bought the place, a few years back.

SON: This is your house now?

ALBERT: Yes, at least – I – want to rebuild it and live here some day –

HEPZIBAH: He says that, but I know he really did it for Mr Johnny and me.

SON: Is Mr Johnny still here?

HEPZIBAH: Of course. (*Calls into the house.*) Mr Johnny! Mr Johnny! Visitors!

MR JOHNNY comes out. He holds out his hand to CARRIE'S SON. His speech is now much clearer than before, but still not crystal clear.

MR JOHNNY: Hello, I'm Johnny Gotobed, pleased to meet you.

SON: Mr Johnny… You can talk!

MR JOHNNY: (*Proud.*) Yes. I see a speech therapist.

HEPZIBAH: Albert paid for him to see a specialist. He's been good to us –

ALBERT: Least I could do. Really.

HEPZIBAH: This is Carrie's son, Mr Johnny. Do you remember little Carrie?

MR JOHNNY: Carrie!

HEPZIBAH: That's right. Can you find us some more eggs? Now we've got extra guests for tea.

MR JOHNNY: Hang on. I'll look.

HEPZIBAH: We'll need five, you see. One for Carrie. She'll be here soon.

MR JOHNNY: I'll get the brown hen's eggs, from the barn.

HEPZIBAH: Yes, you do that. Thank you, Mr Johnny.

MR JOHNNY: (*To CARRIE'S SON.*) Bye bye. See you later.

MR JOHNNY exits.

HEPZIBAH: He'll be so pleased to see Carrie –

SON: Yes, but – I'm sorry, but Mum's not here. She's gone back to the town. I can go and get her if you like –

HEPZIBAH: No need. She'll be here in two minutes – and here am I, talking as if eggs cooked themselves! You two wait here for her –

SON: But she –

HEPZIBAH: When she gets here, tell her that her egg's on the boil, and Hepzibah's waiting. (*Smiles at CARRIE'S SON.*) And that all's well.

HEPZIBAH exits.

SON: (*To ALBERT.*) She really isn't coming, you know. I mean, she will, when I tell her, but she's not coming now. She's too afraid. I hate to disappoint Hepzibah –

ALBERT: So you should. Did Carrie tell you she's a witch?

SON: Yeah, but she's not a proper witch. There's no such thing. Is there?

ALBERT: I would say, Hepzibah's just a very wise woman who's good at guessing.

SON: Well, she's guessed wrong this time.

Unseen by CARRIE'S SON, CARRIE enters.

ALBERT: Hello, Carrie.

CARRIE: Albert Sandwich. What are you doing here?

ALBERT: Waiting for my tea. You're late. By about thirty years.

A moment. Then ALBERT gives CARRIE a half-smile.

CARRIE: Oh, shut up, Albert Sandwich!

CARRIE hugs ALBERT fiercely. He returns the hug with interest. Her SON watches, rather nonplussed.

SON: (*To CARRIE.*) I thought you'd gone. Why did you come back?

CARRIE: Because it's a waste of time, being afraid. (*Looks at ALBERT. With a mischievous smile.*) Come on. Let's go and see Hepzibah and Mr Johnny.

ALBERT picks up CARRIE's suitcase for her. She smiles at him, and picks up ALBERT's suitcase. Carrying their baggage, ALBERT, CARRIE and CARRIE'S SON exit together.

CHOIR: Hwyr a bore fy nymuniad
Esgyn ar adenydd cân
Ar i Dduw, er mwyn fy Ngheidwad
Roddi imi galon lân.

Calon lân yn llawn daioni
Tecach yw na'r lili dlos
Dim ond calon lân all ganu
Canu'r dydd a chanu'r nos.

The End.

Translations Of Welsh Dialogue

PAGE 21–2

MR RHYS: Rhaid i bawb aberthu! Ma pawb o ni yn y rhyfel hwn.

> [Everyone has to make sacrifices. We're all in this war together.]

MRS DAVIES: Dim rhyfel *ni*, yw hwn!

> [This *isn't* our war!]

MR RHYS:Duw, duw! Rhyfel Prydain iw hwn, rhaid i bawb neud eu gorau!

> [Tch! (lit: "God, God!") Britain is at war, everyone has to do their part.]

PAGE 28–9

MR EVANS: Lou! Lou! Ble yn y byd ti wedi mynd nawr?

> [Where in the world have you gone now?]

LOU: O, paid a bod yn grac. Dwi wedi blino, Samuel.

> [Oh don't be angry. I'm tired, Samuel.]

MR EVANS: Iesu mawr! Wedesi un evacuee, a be sy dani? Dau evacuee!

> [Jesus Christ! I said one evacuee and what have we got? Two evacuees!]

MR EVANS: Be ti'n meddwl bo ti'n neud fenyw! Bachgen, bachgen! Gofyn i ti neud un peth, un peth syml. A beth ti wedi neud? Cawlwch!

> [What do you think you're doing, woman? Boy, boy! I ask you to do one thing, one simple thing, and what do you do? You make a mess!]

PAGE 68-9

MR EVANS: (*To LOU.*) Sit down. Cau'r drws. Steddu lawr.

> [Close the door. Sit down.]

MR EVANS: Granda nawr!

> [Listen!]

MR EVANS: Dawnsio! Dawnsio!

> [Dance! Dance!]

LOU: Dim ond am un noson, Samuel!

> [It's only for one night, Samuel!]

MR EVANS: Byth, byth! Tra bod ti'n byw gyda fi!

    [Never! Never! Not whilst you live with me!]

LOU: (*In tears.*) Pam os rhaid i ti sbwlio popeth?

    [Why do you have to spoil everything?]

MR EVANS: Cer i olchi dy wyneb.

    [Go and wash your face.]

Thanks to Rachel Isaac and Siôn Tudor Owen for additional Welsh dialogue.

BACKGROUND MATERIAL AND ACTIVITIES

NINA BAWDEN AND *CARRIE'S WAR*

Childhood and Evacuation

Nina Bawden was born in London in 1925; her maiden name was Nina Mabey. Her father was a marine engineer. The family were not poor, but, according to Nina, 'no one's job was secure in those days', and so her father 'had a fear of poverty that affected all of us'. Nina's mother saw education as a way to ensure her daughter's future and, at the age of 11, Nina found herself under a great deal of pressure to succeed in a scholarship examination for the local grammar school.

Nina Bawden's memory of how responsibility can weigh on a young girl informs the character of evacuee Carrie Willow, charged with looking after her little brother Nick, in *Carrie's War*.

Fortunately, Nina succeeded in gaining her scholarship to Ilford County High School. She studied there until the outbreak of World War 2, when, like many other British children, she was evacuated to the country. At first, Nina went to Ipswich, but after Hitler's invasion of the Low Countries, her school was moved to Wales. Nina and her friend Jean stayed for a week with a miner's family in Blaengarw, South Wales, but were then moved to the larger town of Aberdare. Nina cried to leave Blaengarw, and her vivid memories of this Welsh town would later inspire the creation of *Carrie's War*.

In 1943, Nina Bawden began her studies at Somerville College, Oxford, alongside Margaret Roberts, later Lady Thatcher. A passionate and committed socialist, Nina was shocked when Margaret announced her intention to join the Conservative Party.

Writing Success

Nina's first novel, *Who Calls the Tune*, a detective story, was published in 1953. She wrote it in secret, 'telling no one what I was doing in case they should laugh at me'. The novel was a success. Other critically acclaimed adult novels followed, and it was not until 1963 that Nina wrote her first children's novel, *The Secret Passage*. Since *The Secret Passage*, Nina Bawden has alternated between writing children's books and adult literary fiction.

In 1972, Nina wrote an adult novel, *Anna Apparent*, about a wartime evacuee who suffers terrible abuse on a Welsh hill farm. After writing *Anna Apparent*, Nina remembered her own experiences as an evacuee in Wales, and began to write *Carrie's War*.

Carrie's War was published in 1973, and, like many of Nina Bawden's books, has never been out of print. It was adapted for television in the 1970s, and was filmed by BBC Wales in 2002. *Carrie's War* won a Phoenix Award in 1993, twenty years after its original publication.

Novels

Nina Bawden's other children's novels include *The Secret Passage* (1963); *The Witch's Daughter* (1966); *A Handful of Thieves* (1967); *The Runaway Summer* (1969); *Squib* (1971); *The Peppermint Pig* (1973, winner, Guardian Fiction Award); *The Finding* (1985); *Keeping Henry* (1988); *The Real Plato Jones* (1994, shortlisted for the W H Smith Mind Boggling Books Award) and *Granny the Pag* (1995, shortlisted for the Carnegie Medal).

Her adult novels include *A Woman of My Age* (1967); *Anna Apparent* (1972); *Afternoon of a Good Woman* (1976, winner, Yorkshire Post Novel of the Year Award), *The Ice House* (1983); *Circles of Deceit* (1987, shortlisted, Booker Prize); *Family Money* (1991, shortlisted, Booker Prize) and *A Nice Change* (1997). There have been several film and television adaptations of Nina Bawden's books. In 2004, Nina Bawden was awarded the Golden Pen for a lifetime's contribution to literature.

EVACUATION

Background

During the First World War, over 1400 British civilians had been killed in bombing raids; first by Zeppelins, then by bomber planes. In the period between the wars, the Air Raid Precautions Committee was set up in order to examine the problems caused by air raids, and to look into the possibility of evacuating the civilian populations of British cities, in the case of future air attacks. In 1925, the Committee's report claimed that it would be impossible to relocate the vital work carried out in major cities, and proposed to separate the population into two groups; workers and 'les bouches inutiles' [useless mouths]. All those who played no part in war work were to be considered 'useless mouths'. This group included elderly people, people with disabilities, pregnant women, nursing mothers and, of course, children. In the event of war, it was deemed advisable to remove these people from British cities and send them to the countryside or overseas. This plan became known first as 'evasion', and then by the familiar name by which we refer to it today – evacuation.

Preparation for Evacuation

By late September 1938, with Britain on the brink of war, plans were made to evacuate two million people from London. Half a million schoolchildren were due to leave on 30 September, when the signing of the Munich Agreement seemingly averted war between Britain and Germany at the last minute (or, at any rate, achieved a postponement of hostilities). The evacuation scheme was called off, and 4000 children who had already been evacuated were able to return to their homes. During the year that followed, as Britain prepared for war, arrangements for the evacuation of civilians became an important part of that preparation.

Each area of Britain was assigned to one of three categories: evacuation, reception and neutral. 'Evacuation' areas, mostly towns and cities, were the most likely targets of bombing raids, and vulnerable civilians such as children were to be given the opportunity to leave. They were to be sent to 'reception' areas (generally rural areas, or smaller towns) which were considered comparatively safe. Neutral areas were neither one nor the other. As war became depressingly inevitable, arrangements were made to begin the evacuation on 1 September 1939. This time, there was no last-minute reprieve. The evacuation went ahead as planned. Two days later, Britain was at war with Germany.

Leaving the Cities

It was the largest mass movement of people in British history. One and a half million people were moved from evacuation to reception areas in a few days. Some were sent under the official government scheme, others made their own private arrangements. Some children, often known as 'seavacuees', were sent overseas for the duration of the war, either by government scheme or by private arrangement. But the majority of children were evacuated to other parts of Britain. They were told to turn up at school with their suitcase, gas mask and enough food to last a day. They were issued with labels bearing their name and school, but were not told where they were going. A 'rehearsal' was carried out on 28 August, and on 1 September, the children were finally on the move.

Most children travelled by train. Some ended up only a few miles from their home towns; others faced a long, crowded journey on a train with no toilet facilities and arrived at their destinations tired, hungry, dishevelled, dirty – and in no state to impress their prospective hosts.

Billeting and Foster Parents

The evacuees were to stay in private houses, known as 'billets'. Billeting Officers had examined all the houses in their area, deciding how many evacuees each householder could be made to take. Those who took in child evacuees were known as 'foster parents', and received small sums of money from the government and/or the children's own parents or guardians. Despite this incentive, many were understandably reluctant to open their houses to complete strangers. But, if you lived in a reception area and were considered to have enough room, taking evacuees was compulsory. Unsurprisingly, this caused a certain amount of resentment, and some evacuees faced prejudice from their hosts before they even arrived. Other hosts, however, were eager to 'do their bit' for the war effort by taking in evacuees. 'CARING FOR EVACUEES IS A NATIONAL SERVICE', read the Government posters, encouraging host families to do their patriotic duty.

Arrival

Many children were so traumatised by the experience of their arrival in a strange town that they resolved to return to London at the first opportunity. Humiliations abounded as the evacuees, in some cases already stigmatised as 'dirty townies', reached their reception areas. It was common for evacuees to be made to wait in a central building such as a town hall whilst prospective hosts came to look them over, picking and choosing those they liked the look of, and discarding the rest. Many towns had been sent too many evacuees for the number of billets available, and 'undesirable' children often faced the shame of being dragged from house to house by a billeting officer, begging for someone to agree to take them in.

Back to the Billet

For some evacuees, worse was to come when they went home with their host families. There are stories of children being made to strip naked in front of their hosts, or of having their heads forcibly shaved, in the efforts to combat the lice which some foster-parents believed their 'townie' guests to be carrying.

But there were positive experiences of evacuation, too. In *Carrie's War*, despite the peculiarities of Mr Evans, Carrie relishes her new-found independence – as did Nina Bawden. Pictures of happy city children enjoying the freedom and fresh air of country living were used to encourage parents to send their children away from the urban areas.

Town and Country

In the late 1930s, before television and travel ironed out cultural differences, regional diversity in Britain was much more extreme than it is today. Many hosts and evacuees struggled to understand each other's unfamiliar accents. In North Wales, some hosts spoke only Welsh, and found themselves initially unable to cope with the influx of English-speaking evacuees from Liverpool. In a climate of mutual distrust, rumours flourished. Evacuees were 'dirty', 'hooligans', slum dwellers, riddled with head lice and ringworm, persistent bedwetters. Whilst some hosts' fears were justified, conversely there were evacuees from comfortable homes who were appalled to find themselves in poor, dirty houses where they might be deprived of familiar luxuries such as indoor toilets. Evacuation caused social upheaval on an extraordinary scale. For millions of British people, it was an unprecedented chance to see how the other half lived.

The Drift Back

For the first year of World War 2, the expected devastating air raids did not happen. During this period, known as the 'Phoney War', many children moved back home. Some were brought back by their parents; others ran away. A government campaign was launched to encourage parents to leave their children in the country. A famous poster of the period shows Hitler whispering the words 'Take them back!' into a mother's ear, above the slogan 'Don't do it, Mother – leave the children where they are.'

When the bombing raids did begin, the devastating impact of the Blitz triggered a second wave of evacuations in 1940. It was now expected that Hitler would invade Britain soon, and many areas in the South were reclassified from reception areas to evacuation areas. There was a third wave in 1944, when the flying bombs began to fall on London. But despite all the dangers, there was always a steady trickle of children returning to urban areas to live with their families. Many people, understandably, could not bear to be parted from their children, and took the attitude that, 'If we die, we die together'. Others believed that the pain of parting from their children was worth it for the sake of their children's safety. Fearing the impact of the deaths of children on the country's morale, the British Government vigorously supported its own policy of evacuation until the end.

Going Home

In 1945, plans were finally put into place for the organised return of evacuees. Naturally, there were ecstatic reunions, but for many the end of evacuation was tinged with sadness. There were children who had been parted from their parents for the entire duration of the war; after six years, it was unsurprising that some now felt closer to their foster families. Parents and children did not always recognise each other, especially if the children had been evacuated overseas. A great many children were sad to leave their foster homes. Some refused to leave. And, of course, for those children who had lost their homes and families in the war, there could be no happy homecoming.

AMERICAN SOLDIERS IN BRITAIN

The USA entered in December 1941, after the bombing of Pearl Harbor. By January 1942, US troops had begun to arrive in Britain. They joined various other groups of Allied soldiers, including troops from Canada, New Zealand, Australia, South Africa, India and other Dominion countries. By the end of 1942, there were nearly a quarter of a million US troops stationed in Britain, and the unparalleled resources of the latest arrivals made an enormous impression on the war-ravaged country.

After three years of rationing, blackout, austerity and, of course, air raids, Britain was a shadow of its former self. There was little food to spare, clothing was dowdy and endlessly recycled, petrol was unobtainable except for vital war work, and luxuries and treats of any kind were rare. All types of resources were diverted into the war effort.

American wages were much higher than those of British soldiers, especially in the lower ranks. American troops were cocooned in camps in which the conditions, compared to those of British soldiers and civilians, were positively luxurious. They had their own newspapers and movies, and the food was plentiful and superior. Clubs were opened for American servicemen only, where troops could enjoy meals, dancing and concerts.

The American soldiers were keen to meet British women, and British women were keen to meet them. British men, however, were not so eager to welcome their American guests. To the British 'Tommies', scarred by the hardships of war, the GIs seemed soft and degenerate. The Americans responded by pointing out that, once again, Britain seemed to be reliant on US help to win a war against Germany.

In an enduring phrase which has come to sum up British resentment of their allies, American soldiers were popularly described as 'Overfed, overpaid, oversexed and over here'. The 'oversexed' part infuriated young British men – how could they compete with the rich Americans' ability to show girls a good time?

This issue became a major concern to both the British and American Governments. Fearing that too many of the 'wrong sort' of woman would attempt to ensnare GIs, the authorities tried to ensure that American soldiers were introduced to 'a better type of English girl'. 'Nice' girls were selected by the Red Cross, the Church and the Women's Voluntary Service, and asked to accompany American soldiers to dances and parties, or to offer them tea in their houses. As one of those 'nice' girls, Nina Bawden invited American soldiers to tea in her rooms in Somerville College, and worked as a waitress in the Red Cross Club.

Like evacuation, the stationing of so many American soldiers in Britain provided a chance for very different people to get to know each other's cultures, and caused social upheaval which would have a great impact on society after the war.

BRITAIN AND THE TRANSATLANTIC SLAVE TRADE

From the beginning of the 16th century, Europeans were enslaving people from Africa and forcing them to work in their colonies abroad. An early British slave trader, John Hawkins, was knighted by Queen Elizabeth I, but Elizabeth herself – like many of her subjects – was understandably appalled at the thought of people being kidnapped and enslaved. A justification for slavery was created – that it was moral to take Africans as slaves because by doing so, their 'masters' were introducing them to 'civilisation' and Christianity. This justification persisted for hundreds of years, as slavers and slave owners continued to profit by degrading other human beings. Most slaves were taken to the colonies, but from the 16th century until the late 18th, there were some African slaves in Britain – although it was later decided that slavery had never been legal on British soil.

In 1771, a slave, James Somerset, who had been bought in Virginia, escaped whilst in Britain. He was recaptured and put aboard a ship bound for Jamaica, but his abolitionist friends discovered his fate and tried to help him. A test case of *habeas corpus* was brought before Lord Chief Justice Mansfield, who declared that slavery was illegal under the laws of England.

This ruling was welcomed by abolitionists and slaves – there were between 14,000 and 15,000 slaves in Britain at that time. However, although Mansfield's ruling had deemed slavery illegal in Britain, British traders continued to kidnap African people and sell them elsewhere. It was not until 1807 that Parliament acted to suppress the slave trade, and outlawed the buying, selling and transporting of slaves. Slavery was finally outlawed in the British colonies in 1834.

For information on modern slavery and what can be done to fight it, visit **www.antislavery.org**

INFORMATION AND ACTIVITIES FOR STUDENTS

History

As fiction, *Carrie's War* supports National Curriculum studies on World War 2 – the Home Front. The themes addressed in *Carrie's War* will be particularly useful background for students studying History at Key Stages 1, 2 and 3.

For example, reading, watching or studying *Carrie's War* links particularly well into Key Stage 2, Unit 9: What was it like for children in the Second World War? Section 3: Why were children evacuated? *Carrie's War* provides insight into the following questions:

- What was the Second World War? When and where did it take place?

- What was the Blitz?

- Why were children evacuated?

- What was it like to be an evacuee?

- What did people eat during the war?

- In what other ways might the war have affected people?

- What were children's experiences of the war?

Class Discussion

After seeing the play, or reading the book, ask the class to share what they've learned about these topics.

Some useful quotes which might help the students:

CARRIE: It was during the war. The government sent the children out of the cities, to escape the bombs. We didn't know where we were going. We were just told to turn up at school with a packed lunch and a change of clothes. Our mother tried to make the best of things. 'It'll be such fun, living in the country! You'll love it, see if you don't.' As if Hitler had arranged the war for our benefit. So we could be sent to live with total strangers. She made it sound like it was all some great big adventure!

-

CARRIE: I don't see why we have to wear these things. I mean, I'm not luggage! I can remember who I am and where I live.

ALBERT: Not if you were dead, you couldn't.

CARRIE: Well, obviously –

ALBERT: That's why we've got them, you know. So that if the train gets bombed, they can identify your body.

•

BILLETING OFFICER: Stand over there – over there – by the wall, with the others – and wait for someone to choose you. Now, we need a nice girl for Mrs Davies – let's see… I'm not sure… Mrs Davies, you might want to take a look at this one.

CARRIE: What's going on?

ALBERT: A sort of cattle market, it seems. Or a slave auction.

NICK: Did she get all the sick off my mouth?

CARRIE: Not quite. Come here. And try to cheer up! No one will want us if you look like that!

•

NICK: Mr Evans is a mean old pig, and it's freezing all the time 'cos he won't ever put the gas on. And we never get meat, he keeps all our meat ration for himself and we just get his leftovers even though he gets money from the government and Mum and Dad – he DOES! – You told me.

•

ALBERT: You almost fell in the horse pond, that's all. It's quite dangerous in the blackout.

•

CARRIE: What's wrong with American soldiers?

MR EVANS: You know what they say. Over paid, over fed, over… And over here. It's a life of luxury in that Camp. Everything laid on for them, handed out on a plate. Food, films, dancing - and now women. Our women.

•

MR RHYS: If you really want to help people, how about joining the Girl Guides?

•

NICK: I'd like to be bombed, it'd be super-exciting.

Class Investigation

- Why does Carrie's mother tell her children that evacuation will be an adventure?

- What is 'the blackout'?

- Why should Carrie join the Girl Guides?

- Would being bombed really be exciting?

- Why does Mr Evans hate American soldiers so much?

- What was the 'meat ration'? How much was it?

- Do the students know anyone who was evacuated, or whose family took in an evacuee, during the war? What were their experiences?

Class Discussion

If you had been a parent in World War 2, would you have sent your children away for their own safety? If war broke out today, would you want to be sent away from your parents?

Reading / Writing / Speaking

CHARACTER WORK

Look at the main characters in *Carrie's War*:

CARRIE WILLOW

'Places change more than people, perhaps. People don't change at all…'

NICK WILLOW

'This is the best tea ever. We never get anything like this from mean old Evans.'

ALBERT SANDWICH

'I hate being a kid! You can never make anything happen, or stop anything bad happening. All you can do is stand there and watch and wait to find out what happens.'

SAMUEL ISAAC EVANS

'I watched my Dad die. Killed by a rock fall. Need never have happened, if the company had given a stuff about safety.'

LOUISA EVANS

'Oh, I'm not scared. Exactly. But I've always – minded him.'

FREDERICK EVANS

'It's a narrow place, this valley, Auntie Dilys. Too narrow for me.'

HEPZIBAH GREEN

'No harm ever comes near the innocent.'

JOHNNY GOTOBED

'Tell a story! Tell a story!'

MRS GOTOBED

'Things are seldom as bad as you think they're going to be. Not when you come to them. So it's a waste of time, being afraid.'

CARRIE'S SON

'You're being weird, you do know that, don't you?'

MR RHYS

'Don't you know there's a war on?'

- What do the characters say about themselves?

- What do other people say about them?

- When are they telling the truth?

- When are they lying to each other?

- When are they lying to themselves?

- At what moments in the story do the characters grow and change?

Characters and Relationships: Ideas for Class Discussion

- The adults all seem to expect Carrie to look after Nick. How does Carrie feel about this? What does Nick feel?

• What sort of person is Albert Sandwich? In what ways is he different from Carrie and Nick?

• What do Mr Evans and Auntie Lou expect the evacuee children to be like? Are they surprised?

• Who is in charge at Druid's Bottom? Hepzibah? Mrs Gotobed? Albert? Mr Johnny? What is unusual about this 'family' and their relationships?

• Why is Mr Evans so hostile towards Mr Johnny? How might people react differently to someone like Mr Johnny today? How much have attitudes changed?

• How do Carrie and Nick react differently to Mr Evans? Which of them is 'right'?

• Who is to blame for the long-standing quarrel between Dilys Gotobed and Mr Evans? Do you ever feel sorry for either of them?

• How does Carrie's Son feel about his mother? How does their relationship compare to Carrie's relationship with her mother? To Carrie's relationship with Nick?

• How have relationships between adults and children changed between the 1940s and the present day?

Letter Writing

CARRIE: All right, you write that. And you send it to Mum. And she'll read it and worry and think about it when she's driving her ambulance, and – Is that what you want? Is it?

During the course of the play, Carrie writes at least three letters to her mother. In every letter, Carrie is careful what she says, as she doesn't want her mother to worry. Writing similar letters will give students a chance to explore subtext:

• Imagine you are an evacuee during World War 2. Write a letter to your parent, guardian or someone you don't want to worry about you. Then write a secret diary entry, in which you tell all about what really happened.

• Imagine there is a war happening now, and you have been sent away from where you live for your own safety. Where would you go? Who would you stay with? What is it like? Write a letter, email or series of text messages to your parents, in which you try to reassure them that everything is all right. Then write a letter, email or series of text messages to your best friend, in which you tell them the truth.

ALBERT: I mean it. You have to write the first letter. And if you don't – I'll know, won't I?

Carrie never does write to Albert, and he's too proud to write first. Students can imagine what might have happened if they had written the letters:

• Imagine you are Carrie, writing to Albert, although you saw the house burn down. Do you mention your fears that he may never get the letter? Do you confess to throwing the skull in the pond? What else do you have to say to him?

• Imagine Albert finally did give in and wrote to Carrie. Write the letter. How long might he have waited? Weeks? Months? Years? Will he make up an excuse for writing? Will he confess that he's hurt that Carrie hasn't written? What else will he say?

Story Writing

Ask the students to write their own stories, inspired by the themes (but not necessarily the plot or characters) of *Carrie's War*. Ask them to choose a line from the play, and use it as the first line of a story or written play. Some suggestions might be:

I once did a terrible thing. The worst thing I've ever done in my life...

Make sure you look after your little brother!

God's creatures, spiders. Just like you and me.

A boy! What did I tell you?

He's a monster! A real life scary monster!

I just want to go home for Christmas!

When I die, tell him that I hadn't forgotten him.

It was her life, you see. Parties and ballgowns.

It was amazing! The most exciting thing I've seen in my life.

Getting used to things doesn't make them any better.

Put the past behind you. It's the best way.

Listening / Drama

HOTSEATING

A popular exercise, used widely in drama training, and by professional actors working on productions. This exercise is suitable for students of a wide range of abilities and ages. Obviously, with older and more advanced students, more sophisticated responses can be expected, but younger students can get a great deal out of it too.

Students are asked to take on the role of one of the characters from *Carrie's War*, and sit in the 'hot seat', where the other students can ask them questions about their lives, which they must answer in character. Questions can be simply factual, but more penetrating questions, which investigate a character's deepest conflicts, are very useful in coming to understand them. Students should remember that characters don't always tell the truth!

Some questions might be answered simply at first, but follow-up questions and discussions might extract some more interesting answers and deeper truths. For example:

Carrie – how do you feel about Albert Sandwich?

Nick – Mr Evans says someone's been stealing his biscuits. Do you know anything about it?

Albert – are you popular at school? Do you have many friends?

Mr Evans – why are you so angry with your sister Dilys?

Auntie Lou – has Mr Evans been a good brother to you?

Mrs Gotobed – why do you love dressing up in ballgowns?

Hepzibah – why do you always look after Mr Johnny, when he's no relation to you?

Mr Johnny – what was your life like before you came to live at Druid's Bottom?

Frederick – what do you plan to do after the war?

You could try asking characters the same question at different points in the story – e.g. how does Carrie feel about Mr Evans when she first meets him? When his sister dies? When she thinks he's stolen the will? At the end of the play?

FURTHER ROLE-PLAYING

The students could act out scenes which don't appear in the play, which might have happened before, after or during the action of the play. For example:

Hepzibah breaks the news to Mr Johnny that they are going to move to Wales.

Carrie's Mother comes to visit and has a private word with Mr Evans and / or Auntie Lou.

Mr Johnny takes Nick on a trip to the mountains to see the baby gulls.

Mr Evans finds out about the will and storms over to Druid's Bottom to confront Hepzibah.

Mr Evans tells Auntie Lou that she is not, under any circumstances, to attempt to see any American soldiers.

Mr Johnny has got into a fight with a farmer's son. The farmer confronts Hepzibah.

Carrie and Nick arrive in Glasgow and are reunited with their mother.

Albert confides in Hepzibah that he is hurt that Carrie has never written to him. She tries to persuade him to write first.

Carrie and/or Nick finally decide to confront Mr Evans and tell him to stop bullying Auntie Lou.

These role-playing exercises could lead on to more general exploration of themes from the play, e.g. being sent away from home, protecting younger siblings, guilt and regret, respecting and appreciating people who are different (e.g. people with learning disabilities and speech impediments) and bullying. Students could discuss the different ways in which adults bully other adults, adults bully children and children bully children. Can children bully adults?

IMPROVISATION

Ask the students to take lines from the play and use them to inspire their own improvised scenes. The stories may have nothing to do with *Carrie's War* or evacuation – but they may still give the students an insight into how the themes of the story are still relevant today. The lines could be used as the first line, or the closing line of a scene, or could be hidden in the middle.

Some examples of lines which could be used:

I don't want to go I don't want to go I don't want to go.

How bad can it be? It's not like you killed anyone, is it?

You're much prettier than her.

Keeping secrets from me – in my own house?

You be quiet, and go to your room, girl!

I won't spy for him! I won't tell him anything!

He's always making her cry.

Do him good to get off his backside for once!

Help! Get him off me! Get him off!

Why didn't you fight? I never thought you'd give up so easily.

I mean it. You have to write the first letter. And if you don't – I'll know, won't I?

WEB LINKS

www.spartacus.schoolnet.co.uk/2WWevacuation.htm

Information about evacuation

www.bbc.co.uk/history/ww2children/home.shtml

More information about evacuation

www.bbc.co.uk/cbbc/yourlife/evacuation/

This is the official site of the recent CBBC reality show which asked several modern children to live as evacuees in order to see how they coped.

www.antislavery.org

A website which promotes human rights and campaigns against slavery. Contains educational material on the forms of slavery which are still going on today.

www.spartacus.schoolnet.co.uk/slavery.htm

More information about the history of slavery

www.noveltheatre.com

The home page of Novel Theatre, producers of *Carrie's War*

ADDITIONAL NOTES, 2010

"No one could be too old for it… Carrie's War *is as vivid and elusive as a good dream."*
- Times Educational Supplement

"Carrie had often dreamed about coming back. In her dreams she was twelve years old again; short, scratched legs in red socks and scuffed, brown sandals, walking along the narrow, dirt path at the side of the railway line to where it plunged down, off the high ridge, through the Druid's Grove. The yew trees in the Grove were dark green and so old that they had grown twisted and lumpy, like arthritic fingers. And in Carrie's dream, the fingers reached out for her, plucking at her hair and her skirt as she ran. She was always running by the end of this dream, running away …"
- **The opening lines of *Carrie's War*, by Nina Bawden**

Carrie Willow returns to the Welsh town to which she was evacuated during World War II – thirty years ago. As she tells her children about her wartime experiences, she explains that, "You don't change, you know, growing older..."

And Carrie hasn't changed. Although she is grown up, with a family of her own, she is still haunted by the "dreadful thing" she did as a child. As her son observes, "you would look at her sometimes and see the fear, holding her still."

Now, after half a lifetime shadowed by guilt and nightmares, is Carrie ready to confront her past?

"Sometimes I am not sure at the beginning on which side a book will fall. And sometimes, publishing a novel as a children's book is a matter of marketing… When I started Carrie's War I had not intended it for children; it was only slowly, as I wrote the first chapter, that I began to see the direction it was taking."
- Nina Bawden, author

Carrie relives the events leading up to her mysterious crime. The story begins as she and her brother Nick are evacuated from London to Wales. *Carrie's War* vividly captures the experience of evacuation – the journey into the unknown, the stress of living with strangers, the distrust, uncertainty and fear – but also the sense of adventure, and the adaptability of children faced with a changing world.

"Carrie's War *is a brilliant snapshot of history as we are able to share the point of view of the children who were sent away during the war - a fascinating insight into a part of life that is easily forgotten amongst the seemingly more important historical events of the time. As a mother, I could not imagine sending my daughter away today not knowing where she was going or who would be looking after her. I am sure the mothers of the day went through terrible turmoil between wanting to keep their children safe and wanting them nearby. I don't think I could have let her go.*
- Ann Micklethwaite, Mrs Fazackerly

But despite its authenticity (Nina Bawden was herself evacuated to Wales during World War II), *Carrie's War* is much more than a lively retelling of the experience of evacuation. When Carrie and Nick get to the unnamed Welsh town which is the setting for most of the story, they are thrown into a new life, peopled with unique and memorable characters – whose lives will also be changed forever as a direct result of the government's policy of evacuation.

Carrie's War is simultaneously a bildungsroman, a ghost story, a mystery, a romance and a piece of social history. Through Carrie's eyes, we witness the life of a small town in the Welsh Valleys coping with the arrival of strangers – first London evacuees, and then American soldiers.

"Carrie's War *is a fascinating account of the personal and unseen stories and journeys that accompany huge world events. Mr Johnny is an ambiguous character, but hopefully more than a conduit for difference or otherness. I hope he can be seen as a full and rounded character, replete with the complexities, vulnerabilities and idiosyncrasies that underlie us all."*
- James Beddard, Mr Johnny

As Carrie faces her own fears, growing up in a time of war with the ever-present threat of bombs and invasion, she also confronts Britain's bloody history, learning about human atrocities from pagan ritual sacrifices to the Slave Trade. Faced with these harsh realities, the magical world of the Druid's Grove offers a partial escape - but the supernatural is also a potential threat. The real and the mystical are constantly interwoven as Carrie struggles to understand the secrets of the people she meets. There's the "old religion" mentioned by Auntie Lou, the witch-like skills of "wise woman" Hepzibah, and, of course, the curse of the skull...

"It appeals to young people, because it's a young person's book, but it also appeals to older people – especially those who have been evacuated in the war and can share their experiences. Nina Bawden writes for children and adults and in this novel, I think she speaks to all ages."
- Andrew Loudon, Director

It's a deceptively simple, surprisingly mature novel. The story is told simply and well from Carrie's point of view, but a world of social and political complexity lurks in the background.

"It's not just Carrie's story, it's Carrie observing the stories of the characters she meets. She's observing a lot of adult relationships."
- Sarah Edwardson, Carrie

Adult characters such as the three Evans siblings are drawn with elegant economy, lovingly shaded and beautifully rounded. In particular, Samuel Isaac Evans evolves – or rather, Carrie's perception of him evolves – from a brutal ogre to a figure of almost tragic stature, a victim of his upbringing, class and times but most particularly of his own inflexibility.

Like all great books, it invites re-reading, and will always reward the reader with an extra nuance or complexity. *Carrie's War* is a story to grow up with and read again and again.

Hopefully, audiences come away from the show having been entertained, challenged and enlightened, and want to go on holiday to Wales! By stepping into the shoes of Carrie, they should share her journey, the extreme circumstances which she finds herself in – and a little of the wisdom she gains along the way.
- James Beddard, Mr Johnny

EVACUATION

In 1939, with Britain on the brink of war with Germany, arrangements were made to evacuate vulnerable civilians from the most dangerous areas – those which were considered the most likely targets for German bombing raids or attempted invasions. "Evacuees" included disabled people, nursing mothers and children.

ALBERT: I hate being a kid! You can never make anything happen, or stop anything bad happening. All you can do is stand there and watch and wait to find out what happens…

Evacuation began on September 1st, 1939. Two days later, Britain was at war with Germany.

"As if Hitler had arranged this old war for their benefit, just so that Carrie and Nick could be sent away in a train with gas masks slung over their shoulders and their names on cards round their necks. Labelled like parcels – Caroline Wendy Willow and Nicholas Peter Willow – only with no address to be sent to."
- Nina Bawden, *Carrie's War*, Chapter One

One and a half million people were moved from Britain's major cities in a few days. Some were sent under the official Government scheme, others made their own private arrangements. A certain number of children, often known as "seavacuees", were sent abroad for the duration of the war, but the majority were evacuated to other parts of Britain. They were told to turn up at school with their suitcase, gas mask and enough food to last a day. They were issued with labels bearing their name and school, but were not told where they were going.

CARRIE: I don't see why we have to wear these things. I mean, I'm not luggage! I can remember who I am and where I live.

ALBERT: Not if you were killed. That's why we've got them. So that if the train gets bombed, they can identify your body.

The evacuees were to stay in private houses, known as "billets". Those who took in child evacuees were known as "foster parents", and received small sums of money from the government and/or the children's own parents or guardians. Taking part in the scheme was compulsory. Billeting officers had examined all the houses in their area, deciding how many evacuees each householder could be made to accommodate.

MR RHYS, THE BILLETING OFFICER: Let's have a bit of respect now! Bit of gratitude. You come down here, expect decent people to take you in - not as if we get a choice in the matter.

Most children travelled by train. Some ended up only a few miles from their home towns; others faced a long, crowded journey on a train with no toilet facilities and arrived at their destinations tired, hungry, dishevelled and dirty.

It was common for the evacuees to be made to wait in a central building such as a town hall whilst prospective hosts came to look them over, picking and choosing those they liked the look of, and discarding the rest.

CARRIE: What's going on?

ALBERT: A sort of cattle market, it seems.

Many towns had been sent too many evacuees for the number of billets available, and some children faced the ordeal of being dragged from house to house by a billeting officer, begging for someone to agree to take them in.

"…she had already begun to feel ill with shame at the fear that no one would choose her, the way she always felt when they picked teams at school. Supposing she was left to the last!"
- Nina Bawden, *Carrie's War*, chapter 2

In the late 1930s, before television and travel ironed out cultural differences, regional diversity in Britain was much more extreme than it is today. Many hosts and evacuees struggled to understand each others' unfamiliar accents:

NICK: He sounds like Hitler!

CARRIE: That's Welsh, not German!

In a climate of mutual distrust, rumours flourished. Householders fretted that they were expected to take in evacuees who were "dirty", "hooligans", slum dwellers, riddled with head lice and ringworm, persistent bedwetters.

LOU: Samuel, the boy's only a babby -

MR EVANS: Not too much of a babby, I hope. I won't have wet beds in this house!

NICK: That's a rude thing to mention.

Whilst some foster parents' fears were justified, conversely there were evacuees from comfortable homes who were appalled to find themselves in poor, dirty houses where they might be deprived of familiar luxuries such as indoor toilets. Whatever the circumstances, host families and evacuees alike struggled to come to terms with living with strangers.

"Carrie saw the marks of their rubber-soled shoes and felt guilty, though it wasn't her fault. Nick whispered, 'She thinks we're poor children, too poor to have slippers', and giggled."
- Nina Bawden, *Carrie's War*, Chapter 2

Evacuation caused social upheaval on an extraordinary scale. For millions of British people, it was an unprecedented chance to see how the other half lived – and there were certainly positive aspects to this experience. Pictures of happy city children, enjoying the freedom and fresh air of country living, were used to encourage parents to send their own children away from the cities. The resilience of youth helped evacuee children to make themselves at home in unfamiliar surroundings; they often picked up local ways, including different regional accents.

"It seemed, in fact, as if they had lived there all their lives long. Slept in that bedroom, eaten in that kitchen, used the earth privy in the daytime (Nick got constipation because of the spiders); kept out of Mr Evans' way; woken up to the pit hooter wailing; gone running to school down the hilly, main street..."
- Nina Bawden, *Carrie's War*, Chapter 3

For the first year of World War II, the expected devastating air raids did not happen. During this period, known as the "Phoney War", many children moved back home. When the bombing raids did begin, the impact of the Blitz triggered a second wave of evacuations in 1940. There was a third wave in 1944, when the flying bombs began to be dropped on London. But despite all the dangers, there was always a steady trickle of children returning to the cities to live with their families.

NICK: I just want to go home for Christmas!

In 1945, plans were finally put into place for the organised return of evacuees. There were ecstatic reunions, but for many the end of evacuation was tinged with sadness. Many children had been parted from their parents for the entire duration of the war, and some now felt closer to their foster families.

"'What's your mother like?' Albert asked.

'Well, she's quite tall', Carrie began, and stopped. Not because she couldn't remember, but because it was such a long time since she'd seen her and she felt strange… She thought, suppose I don't recognise her, suppose she doesn't recognise me…"

- Nina Bawden, *Carrie's War*, chapter 13

A great many children were sad to leave their foster homes. Some even refused to go. And, of course, for those children who had lost their homes and families in the war, there could be no happy homecoming.

Emma Reeves, 2010